New Perspectives on Turkey-EU Relations

This book makes the case for looking afresh at Turkey-EU relations in order to appreciate the richness and complexity of a relationship which is now more than 50 years old and is still not close to reaching fulfilment. The contributors challenge conventional attempts to understand Turkey-EU relations, revealing that EU integration studies has been rather poor at understanding the global context within which Turkey-EU developments take place. More surprising perhaps, EU integration studies has also struggled to give sufficient weight to the potential of Turkey's domestic politics to shape EU enlargement. The volume attempts to correct these imbalances by offering both a global context and new perspectives on the drivers of domestic politics. It represents a shift from a narrow EU integration/enlargement agenda. Turkey's position vis-a-vis the EU cannot be adequately captured by simplistic notions of conditionality, harmonization, and an uncritical interpretation of Europeanization. A more rounded view of Turkey-EU relations is advanced based upon a broader context of European and global transformations. The contributions, collected here, offer an interpretation of Turkey-EU relations from a novel perspective, utilize a new framework of theory, and draw upon insights and perspectives from disciplines underrepresented in mainstream study of Turkey-EU relations.

This book was published as a special issue of the *Journal of Contemporary European Studies*.

Chris Rumford is Professor of Political Sociology and Global Politics at Royal Holloway, University of London where he is also Director of the Centre for Global and Transnational Politics. He is also a member of the editorial board of the *Journal of Contemporary European Studies*. His research interests include Turkey-EU relations, Europe's shifting borders, globalization theory, cosmopolitanism, and the politics of cricket.

New Perspectives on Turkey-EU Relations

Edited by
Chris Rumford

LONDON AND NEW YORK

First published 2013
by Routledge

2 Park Square, Milton Park, Abingdon, Oxfordshire OX14 4RN
711 Third Avenue, New York, NY 10017

Routledge is an imprint of the Taylor & Francis Group, an informa business

First issued in paperback 2018

Copyright © 2013 Taylor & Francis

This book is a reproduction of the *Journal of Contemporary European Studies*, vol. 19/issue 4. The Publisher requests to those authors who may be citing this book to state, also, the bibliographical details of the special issue on which the book was based.

All rights reserved. No part of this book may be reprinted or reproduced or utilised in any form or by any electronic, mechanical, or other means, now known or hereafter invented, including photocopying and recording, or in any information storage or retrieval system, without permission in writing from the publishers.

Notice:
Product or corporate names may be trademarks or registered trademarks, and are used only for identification and explanation without intent to infringe.

British Library Cataloguing in Publication Data
A catalogue record for this book is available from the British Library

ISBN13: 978-0-415-82571-9 (hbk)
ISBN13: 978-1-138-37774-5 (pbk)

Typeset in Times New Roman
By Taylor & Francis Books

Publisher's Note
The publisher would like to make readers aware that the chapters in this book may be referred to as articles as they are identical to the articles published in the special issue. The publisher accepts responsibility for any inconsistencies that may have arisen in the course of preparing this volume for print.

Contents

Citation Information — vii
Notes on Contributors — ix

1. Introduction: New Perspectives on Turkey–EU Relations
   Chris Rumford — 1

2. Constructing Turkey Inc.: The Discursive Anatomy of a Domestic and Foreign Policy Agenda
   Nora Fisher Onar — 5

3. Ombudsmanship and Turkey's Europeanization in 'World Society'
   Didem Buhari-Gulmez — 17

4. Resisting Anamnesis: A Nietzschean Analysis of Turkey's National History Education
   Edward Webb — 31

5. A Bakhtinian Approach to EU–Turkey Relations
   Johanna Nykänen — 43

6. Turkey's Path to EU Membership: An Historical Institutionalist Perspective
   Gulay Icoz — 53

7. Kurdish Transnational Politics and Turkey's Changing Kurdish Policy: The Journey of Kurdish Broadcasting from Europe to Turkey
   Bilgin Ayata — 65

8. The Post-westernisation of EU–Turkey Relations
   Hasan Turunç — 77

Index — 89

Citation Information

The following chapters were originally published in the *Journal of Contemporary European Studies,* volume 19, issue 4 (December 2011). When citing this material, please use the original page numbering for each article, as follows:

Chapter 1
Editorial: New Perspectives on Turkey–EU Relations
Chris Rumford
Journal of Contemporary European Studies, volume 19, issue 4 (December 2011) pp. 459-462

Chapter 2
Constructing Turkey Inc.: The Discursive Anatomy of a Domestic and Foreign Policy Agenda
Nora Fisher Onar
Journal of Contemporary European Studies, volume 19, issue 4 (December 2011) pp. 463-474

Chapter 3
Ombudsmanship and Turkey's Europeanization in 'World Society'
Didem Buhari-Gulmez
Journal of Contemporary European Studies, volume 19, issue 4 (December 2011) pp. 475-488

Chapter 4
Resisting Anamnesis: A Nietzschean Analysis of Turkey's National History Education
Edward Webb
Journal of Contemporary European Studies, volume 19, issue 4 (December 2011) pp. 489-500

Chapter 5
A Bakhtinian Approach to EU–Turkey Relations
Johanna Nykänen
Journal of Contemporary European Studies, volume 19, issue 4 (December 2011) pp. 501-510

CITATION INFORMATION

Chapter 6
Turkey's Path to EU Membership: An Historical Institutionalist Perspective
Gulay Icoz
Journal of Contemporary European Studies, volume 19, issue 4 (December 2011) pp. 511-522

Chapter 7
Kurdish Transnational Politics and Turkey's Changing Kurdish Policy: The Journey of Kurdish Broadcasting from Europe to Turkey
Bilgin Ayata
Journal of Contemporary European Studies, volume 19, issue 4 (December 2011) pp. 523-534

Chapter 8
The Post-westernisation of EU–Turkey Relations
Hasan Turunç
Journal of Contemporary European Studies, volume 19, issue 4 (December 2011) pp. 535-546

Notes on Contributors

Bilgin Ayata is Assistant Professor at the Political Science Department of Freie Universität Berlin, Germany. Previously she was a Postdoctoral Fellow at the 'The Transformative Power of Europe' research group at the Freie Universität. She holds a PhD in Political Science from Johns Hopkins University, Baltimore and an MA in Political Science from York University, Canada.

Didem Buhari-Gulmez studied International Relations at the Middle East Technical University, the University of Edinburgh, and the University of London. From September 2013 she will be an Early Career Research Fellow at Oxford Brookes University. Her publications on world polity and Turkey-European Union relations have appeared in *International Political Sociology*, *Journal of Contemporary European Studies*, *South East European and Black Sea Studies*, and *New Global Studies*.

Gulay Icoz is a PhD candidate in the Department of Politics and International Relations, Royal Holloway, University of London. She holds an MRES in European Politics from Birkbeck College, University of London, and a BA in Politics from Goldsmiths College, University of London. Since 2006 she has been a Local Councillor in the London Borough of Hackney.

Johanna Nykänen is a PhD candidate at the University of Warwick. She was previously a Research Assistant in the EU research programme at the Finnish Institute of International Affairs and a visiting researcher at Bogazici University, Turkey. She holds an MA in Central and South-East European Studies from University College London.

Nora Fisher Onar holds a DPhil (Oxford University), a Masters (Johns Hopkins—SAIS) and a Bachelor's (Georgetown—SFS) degree in International Relations. She has published extensively on Turkish politics and the rise of non-western actors in fora like *Middle East Studies* and *Women's Studies International Forum*, and edited volumes for OUP, CUP, I. B. Tauris and Routledge.

Chris Rumford is Professor of Political Sociology and Global Politics at Royal Holloway College, London, Director of the Centre for Global and Transnational Politics and a member of the editorial board of the *Journal of Contemporary European Studies*. His new book 'The Globalization of Strangeness' was published by Palgrave in 2013.

NOTES ON CONTRIBUTORS

Hasan Turunç is a visiting scholar at the School of Interdisciplinary Area Studies, University of Oxford, and a Research Associate at Foreign Policy Centre. His forthcoming book 'The Democratic Transition in Turkey: The Transformation of Civil Society and the Challenges of EU Accession' (I. B. Tauris) investigates Turkey – European politics beyond dichotomies: West/East, modern/traditional, global/local and secular/Islamicist.

Edward Webb is Assistant Professor of Political Science & International Studies at Dickinson College, in Pennsylvania. He has a BA in Oriental Studies from Cambridge University, and an MA and PhD in Political Science from the University of Pennsylvania. A former diplomat, his research and teaching interests include comparative politics of Turkey and the Middle East, in particular secularism, authoritarianism and the politics of education.

Introduction: New Perspectives on Turkey-EU Relations

Introduction

This special thematic issue of the *Journal of Contemporary European Studies* deals with a familiar topic—Turkey–EU relations—but approaches it in a variety of different ways. The underlying idea is that we need to look at Turkey and the EU afresh in order to appreciate the richness and complexity of a relationship which is now more than fifty years old (a fact alone that suggests no ordinary relationship) and is still not close to reaching fulfilment (Cakir, 2011). To this end, the articles collected here challenge conventional attempts to understand Turkey–EU relations. They reveal that EU integration studies has been rather poor at developing a global context (or even demonstrating a global awareness). More surprising perhaps integration studies has also struggled to give sufficient weight to the potential of Turkey's domestic politics to shape EU enlargement. Taken together, the seven articles contained in this issue attempt to correct these imbalances by offering both a global context and new perspectives on the drivers of domestic politics.

The development of the EU, its enlargement and future trajectory is often conveyed in developmental and/or quasi-teleological terms. EU integration is seen as the destiny for the continent and each country (including non-members) is compelled to seek a place in the unfolding order. Turkey's attempt to slot into the EU project is generally viewed as having been unsuccessful, for one of two interrelated reasons. The first is that the EU has been guilty of 'shifting the goalposts' in respect of Turkey's accession criteria. The second is that Turkey has found it impossible to hit the moving target represented by the EU's changing accession criteria either because of a blatant (at times) refusal to conform to EU requirements (protection of minorities, human rights) or because of Turkey's rather inadequate assessments of the opportunity for EU accession, such as still seeking Customs Union in the 1990s while former Warsaw Pact countries were negotiating accession agreements: what has been termed, 'Ankara Agreement Syndrome' (Öniş, 2000).

The articles here represent a shift away from a narrow EU integration agenda. Turkey's position vis-à-vis the EU cannot be adequately captured by simplistic notions of conditionality, harmonization and an uncritical interpretation of Europeanization. The argument here is that an EU integration studies agenda will only tell part of the Turkey–EU story. What is required in order to provide a fuller account is a more rounded view of Turkey–EU relations, one which places it in a broader context of European and global transformations. This special thematic issue advances a European studies interpretation of Turkey–EU relations and as such offers a much needed alternative to the dominant interpretations emanating from EU integration studies. What distinguishes this European studies approach?

First, European studies offers greater multidisciplinarity. Whereas integration studies tends to be dominated by political scientists and international relations scholars European studies embraces a host of disciplinary perspectives. The broadening of the field (in this volume) to include contributions from sociology, cultural studies, linguistics and education provides much more variety than is usually the case with integration studies. Too often, EU integration studies insists that if other disciplines wish to participate they must do so by following an agenda framed by political scientists, and in fact it is often the case that scholars in these disciplines are happy to participate on these terms (Favell & Guiraudon, 2011).

Second, European studies poses a broader range of questions about Europe. European studies deals primarily with the transformation of Europe, of which EU integration is one part. European studies is centrally concerned with the question of cultural identities, of Europe's relation to the rest of the world, of transnational communities, of cross-border mobilities and networks, of colonial legacies and of the heritage of a multiplicity of European peoples. The argument here is this is a potentially productive context within which to study Turkey–EU relations. European studies aims to study Europe in the broadest and most inclusive sense possible and it should never presume to be able to answer the question 'What is Europe?' in definitive, once-and-for-all terms (Biebuyck & Rumford, forthcoming).

Third, understanding Europe's changing role in world politics needs to be prioritized. Caricaturing EU studies we can say that it has been rather inward-looking and tends to see Europe as separate from the rest of the world. European studies encourages approaches to studying Europe that place it within a global framework. European studies is concerned with exploring the transformations which have shaped and continue to shape Europe, both internally and in the wider world.

The Articles

The articles which comprise this thematic special issue each contribute to the European studies agenda by offering an interpretation of Turkey–EU relations from a novel perspective or by utilizing a new framework of theory, or by drawing upon insights and perspectives from disciplines underrepresented in mainstream study of Turkey–EU relations.

Nora Fisher Onar draws upon speech act theory in her paper 'Constructing Turkey Inc.' in order to illuminate the foreign and domestic policy choices of Turkey's ruling AK Party. This highlights a key theme common to several of the articles: the need to pay much more attention to the dynamics of domestic politics in Turkey, which is much more influential than often thought in shaping the course of Turkey–EU relations. Fisher Onar is particularly concerned to understand the apparent contradictions in AKP's position as revealed in the party's discourses of democracy, Islam and Ottomanism, and the titular 'Turkey Inc.' an attempt to constitute Turkey as a soft power hub. Fisher Onar finds that these discourses are not contradictory but are designed to appeal to different constituencies of support. The article makes an important and original contribution to understanding AKP as much more than a party with 'Islamic leanings.'

Didem Buhari-Gulmez utilizes globalization theory, in the form of 'world polity theory' alternatively known as the Stanford School's sociological institutionalism, in order to investigate the link between Europeanization and globalization. Her exploration of ombudsmanship in Turkey, the first time such a study has been attempted, places Turkey's relationship with the EU in the context of 'world society'. She finds, contrary to received wisdom, that global culture is driving Europeanization, and that Europe itself is being constructed globally. This important contribution not only places Turkey within 'world society' but also offers a particularly sophisticated reading of the way Europe is being shaped by global forces.

Adopting a Nietzschean approach, Ed Webb, in his article 'Resisting anamnesis', investigates Turkey's selective teaching of national history in schools. The curriculum, as established under Ataturk focuses on ancient Turks, the Ottomans, Enlightenment Europe and the establishment of the Republic. It stops at the Second World War. Turkey's history as a democracy punctuated by coups, its experiences as a member of NATO, the rise of political Islam and Kurdish nationalism are all outside the curriculum. In this original analysis Webb contextualizes the self-conscious deployment of history by Turkey's elites and highlights the role of forgetting in this construction of history.

Drawing upon a very different philosophical tradition, Johanna Nykänen offers a Bakhtinian reading of EU–Turkey relations. Bakhtin's concept of dialogism is deployed as a basis for arguing that Turkey should not be passive, like many previous candidate countries, in its dealings with the EU. Essentially, Turkey should be able to 'talk back', to the EU. In this way, a genuine and meaningful dialogue between Turkey and the EU can be established. Nykänen makes explicit a theme which is also present in other contributions; that Turkey–EU relations are normally assumed to consist of 'one way traffic', with the EU as sender and Turkey as receiver of directives and requirements for political, economic and social change. Nykänen reveals the limitations of these assumptions and outlines the advantages that greater dialogue could bring.

Gulay Icoz offers an original interpretation of Turkey–EU relations from a 'Historical Institutionalist' perspective, a framework hitherto not utilized in Turkey–EU scholarship. She outlines how the Historical Institutionalist concepts of 'path dependence' and 'punctuated equilibrium' reveal the importance of domestic political institutions, particularly the National Security Council (MGK), in determining the trajectory of Turkey–EU relations. The strength of this article lies in the re-interpretation of familiar historical episodes and the shift in the locus of Turkey–EU studies which is required to understand the forces shaping Turkey's EU candidature.

Bilgin Ayata demonstrates that transnational politics can have an important influence on domestic policy choices. She investigates the way in which the Kurdish diaspora, particularly the political entrepreneurs behind Kurdish broadcasting, has shaped Turkey's policy towards the Kurds. She demonstrates that Turkey's decision to offer a domestic TV channel broadcasting in Kurdish is a response to transnational media activism. In a bold analysis Ayata demonstrates that the motor of policy choices and political change may be located beyond national borders (and not necessarily driven by EU interests).

Hasan Turunc locates Turkey–EU relations within the broader context of global social and political transformations. Working with the concept of 'post-westernization' he seeks to challenge orthodox interpretations of Turkey's EU vocation by exploring the limitation of accounts based on dichotomies and cleavages: East/West, traditional/modern, secular/Islam. Turunc demonstrates a command of both the detail of domestic politics and the broad sweep of global transformations. Understanding the post-westernization of EU–Turkey relations is revealed as the key to understanding both Turkey's changing place in Europe, and Europe's role in the world.

In addition to the thematic set of articles, this issue also contains an article by Jeanne Fagnani and Antoine Math on child care policies in France. The authors argue that, for all the rhetoric devoted to the promotion of 'freedom of choice' for parents in the French childcare sector, evidence suggests a different set of priorities; namely a primary desire to bring more mothers into the workforce while at the same time satisfying the increasing demands placed on employees through the development of flexible work schedules and in particular non-standard work hours.

The issue is rounded off with a sizeable set of book reviews.

Chris Rumford

References

Biebuyck, W. & Rumford, C. (forthcoming, 2012) Many Europes: rethinking multiplicity. *European Journal of Social Theory*.
Cakir, A. E. (Ed.) (2011) *Fifty Years of EU–Turkey Relations: A Sisyphean Story* (Basingstoke: Palgrave).
Favell, A. & Guiraudon, V. (2011) *Sociology of the European Union* (Basingstoke: Palgrave).
Öniş, Z. (2000) *Luxembourg, Helsinki and Beyond: Towards an Interpretation of Recent Turkey–EU Relations*. Paper presented at the annual Conference of the British Society for Middle Eastern Studies (BRISMES), University of Cambridge, England, 2–5 July.

Constructing Turkey Inc.: The Discursive Anatomy of a Domestic and Foreign Policy Agenda

NORA FISHER ONAR*
Bahçeşehir University, Istanbul, Turkey

ABSTRACT *The article draws on speech act theory to argue that Turkey's ruling Justice and Development Party (AKP) wields a discursive repertoire that consists of four main narratives: a democratization, a (post-)Islamist, an Ottomanist and a Turkey Inc. story. It examines the illocutionary intent, that is, the ways in which discourses are used to co-ordinate policy and strategically project appeals to specific constituencies. It also examines the perlocutionary uptake of these discourses, namely, the ways in which they are received by target audiences. This makes it possible to unpack the tensions which obtain within and across narratives, and account for the apparent contradictions in AKP positions on a range of issues. The overarching argument of the article is that the party's prime purpose is to establish Turkey Inc., that is to position Turkey as a (soft) power hub and gateway for transactions across its multiple regions and hinterlands, the other discourses in the repertoire, the article contends, are harnessed to this end.*

Introduction

In the past decade, Turkey has undergone a dramatic transformation. The secularist elite that controlled the country since its foundation in 1923 has been displaced by a new establishment representing formerly peripheral elements under the leadership of the pro-religious Justice and Development Party (*Adalet ve Kalkınma Partisi* AKP). In addition to controlling the Government, the parliament, and the presidency, and dislodging the military from its longstanding custodianship of the national project, the party recently received a mandate from 58 per cent of the electorate to pursue constitutional reform. This will permit it—*inter alia*—to transform the last bastion of the old elite, the judiciary. Meanwhile, EU accession-oriented reforms undertaken in the first half of the 2000s have opened the door to vigorous debates on once taboo topics like the domestic Kurdish and Armenian questions. A pro-active foreign policy agenda has also served the cause of rapprochement with formerly problematic neighbours such as Greece, Syria and Iran, and unprecedented if unconsummated activism in relations with Nicosia and Yerevan. AKP success has also been a function of a booming economy. In the wake of IMF-instituted structural reforms, Turkey has averaged 6 per cent growth and attracted up to 20 billion dollars investment per year, up from a scant billion in the 1990s. This has enabled it to climb the ranks of the G20, with some analysts anticipating the country will have the world's tenth largest economy by 2050 (The Economist, 2010a). The political and economic transformation—perhaps most palpable in rising urban hubs across Anatolia—has given a heightened sense of confidence to much of the population. In their view, Turkey finally appears to be fulfilling the proverbial 'potential' about which observers of the country waxed, unrequited, for decades.

Others are disconcerted by the altered state of affairs. These include many within the old elite and their interlocutors in American and European policy circles. Quietude is also discernible among groups whose aspirations mesh at best awkwardly with those of the AKP such as secular/nationalist Kurds, heterodox Alevis, gays and lesbians and the dwindling non-Muslim communities. Ambivalence emanates from at least two sources. One is anxiety over the fate of secularism given the pro-religious orientation of the ruling party and its electorally hegemonic constituency. The second, inter-related concern is over Turkey's trajectory and the depth of AKP commitment to the West. Though the AKP has sought to assuage such fears, its habit of mixing democratic, conservative-religious, Ottomanist and mercantilist metaphors has left many observers confused.

This tableau has sent observers scrambling for a turn-of-phrase to capture the substance of Turkey's transformation and assess its promise and challenges. One label is 'neo-Ottomanism' which flags the fact that AKP-led Turkey is embracing the Ottoman past as inspiration for a more pluralistic but also more conservative domestic order on one hand, and a pro-active, multi-regional foreign policy towards former Ottoman territories on the other (Fisher Onar, 2009a, 2009b). A second trope suggests that Turkey is 'switching axes', that is, abandoning its longstanding commitment to the West in favour of the East, especially the Islamic world. This formula resonates with those disturbed by Turkey's outreach to neighbours like Syria and Iran and the concomitant downturn in Turkish–Israeli relations. While such frames shed light on aspects of Turkey's transformation—and the anxieties it engenders—they are far from sufficient. One reason is simply because the AKP rejects both labels. It eschews the term 'neo-Ottomanism' because of its neo-imperial connotations, and refutes the claim that Turkey has turned eastwards because this discounts the possibility of multiple commitments. The alacrity with which many a commentator has embraced these frames nevertheless suggests they may become self-fulfilling prophecies.

It is thus urgent that we develop a more nuanced framework with which to take stock of the emerging situation. A constructivist approach is well suited to the task as it can help us identify, unpack and understand the interface between what—I will contend—are multiple threads of AKP activism. Such a framework may be derived from speech act theory first developed by linguists and intellectual historians like Austin, Searle, Skinner and Pocock, and which has informed the work of constructivists engaged in domestic and foreign policy analysis such as Doty, Weldes, Larsen, Waever, Risse-Kaplan, Sikkink and Kazenstein, to name but a few. These works draw on the insight that policy actors' utterances are more than words which convey meaning but *illocutionary* acts which serve two prime functions.

The first is to reflect the bundle of common understandings that constitute the worldview of the speaker and the community in which s/he is embedded. As such, history—a shared history—matters in terms of furnishing the building blocks of a discourse. For the act of communication will always entail 'the taking up of some determinate position in relation to some pre-existing conversation or argument' (Skinner, 2002, p. 115). In this article, I will show that at least four experiences have served as constitutive moments in the political tradition of which the AKP is the latest incarnation. The first was the transition from Ottoman-Islamic empire to republican nation-state in which religious subjectivity was forcibly displaced to the private sphere; the second was the centre-right tradition inaugurated by the Democrat Party (DP) with the transition to multi-party politics in 1950; the third was the political Islamist tradition of the National View (MG) movement founded by Necmettin Erbakan in the late 1960s; and, the fourth was secularist suppression of the MG in 1997 which engendered receptivity to EU/European referents for democratization.

A second feature of illocutionary acts regards intent. That is, they reflect the speaker's strategic assessment of the demands of audience and context. As such, policy discourses are neither written in stone, nor need they be internally consistent. Rather, they evolve over time and are interpreted in variegated ways. Thus, a political party like the AKP may espouse a range of narratives at any given time, and each strand may display tensions both internally and vis-à-vis the other strands. Contradictions may be amplified when the party mixes metaphors in light of the imperative of the moment and the target audience(s). By recognizing this, we can begin to make sense of the apparent inconsistencies in AKP discourses of which there are, I suggest, at least four. These are a *democratization* narrative, a *(post-)Islamist* narrative, an *Ottomanist* narrative and a story which I call *Turkey Inc.*

To understand the consequences—intended or otherwise—which illocutionary acts may engender it is also necessary to assess their *perlocutionary* effects or the 'uptake' of the speech act by audiences. For policy-makers cannot ensure that their understanding of and intention in staking a discursive position will align with its reception. Audience responses may entail reflection, refraction, distortion, or even transformation of the meaning and agenda of the speaker, in turn, shaping the parameters of the speaker's next illocutionary act. The probability of mismatch between illocution and perlocution is all the more salient in an era of heightened globalization and instantaneous mass communication in which it is difficult to segregate audiences. Thus, tensions already embedded in and across narratives can pique powerful and unexpected reactions when audiences overlap. In the case of the AKP, I will show that when (post-)Islamist metaphors are invoked either exclusively or in tandem with other strands and when the audience includes western as well as Middle Eastern actors, then outcomes can be explosive. Turkish–Israeli clashes at Davos and over Gaza are cases in point. Yet, I will go on to argue, the driving story, at least for the time being, is Turkey Inc., an interest rather than ideology-driven agenda in the service of which the other strands are co-opted. Recognizing this may provide a platform for Turkey's allies in the West to rewrite their relations with transformed Turkey in a win–win fashion.

The AKP Repertoire

The Democratization Story

The vision of democratization articulated by AKP figures is clearly informed by the DP centre-right tradition and the experience of repression on the part of secularist actors in the late 1990s. The DP and its charismatic leader Adnan Menderes subscribed to a *laissez-faire* ideology in their economic policies and political rhetoric. Their understanding of democracy was majoritarian and populist and—over the course of their decade in power—increasingly erratic in its commitment to the freedoms of non-constituents. Meanwhile, in the name of religious freedom, they relaxed early republican proscriptions on public religiosity, instituting religious curricula in secondary schools and legalizing banned religious sects. Such moves piqued fears for the secularist cultural revolution and contributed to the enactment by a group of junior officers of Turkey's first military coup in 1960. The upshot was an enduring reserve domain for the army. The execution of Menderes and two deputies in the context of the coup represents a moment of transcendental violence for pro-religious elements and engendered deep aversion for the military guardians of Turkish secularism. Such sentiments were renewed on 28 February 1997—a date of neuralgic resonance for pro-religious cohorts—when the army released a memorandum chastising then prime minister Erbakan for anti-secularist activities. This unleashed a process that culminated in his party's closure and the censure of actors from across pro-religious civil society. The experience spurred such actors in the late 1990s and early 2000s to seek vindication via the democratic norms and values touted by the EU.

Such sources furnish the building blocks and of the AKP democratization narrative which is projected for the most part towards domestic audiences and interlocutors in Europe and to a lesser extent the United States. One key element is the notion of the 'people' (*halk*) which the AKP equates with its own pro-religious constituency in juxtaposition to those it characterizes as secularist 'elites' (*seçkinler*). Prime Minister Recep Tayyip Erdoğan's working class roots are often invoked in this regard. The trope is employed in the build-up to national and municipal elections though the AKP never actually carried a majority of the electorate until the 12 September 2010 referendum on constitutional reform. In such campaigns, pro-secular opponents are often portrayed as parasitic autocrats beholden to a superficial westernism which they are said to employ in order to exploit the hardworking, pious masses. This discursive strategy strips secularist cadres of their authenticity, enabling the representatives of the 'real' Turkey to dismiss concerns articulated by pro-secular figures.

At the same time, the democratization narrative is replete with suggestions that the 'people' preferences are aligned with EU/European standards and values. Thus, in the campaign leading up to the recent referendum, billboards across the country urged citizens to vote 'yes' to 'European' benchmarks in all walks of life, from civil–military relations to retirement benefits. Even the choice of date—12 September—was significant in that it marked the twentieth anniversary of the 1980 coup, the constitutional legacy of which the AKP was seeking a mandate to transform. When, however, relations with the EU are rocky, the referent may shift. For instance, in the mid-2000s—a time when EU reticence on Turkish accession was becoming transparent—AKP pundits preferred to invoke 'universal' values for principles they had previously flagged as 'European'. They also used this elision in dialogue with and critique of EU counterparts. As Minister of State Mehmet Şahin put it, 'You cannot say these values are universal and then expect them to apply only to yourselves.'[1] Yet, another strategy has been to indigenization, evident in the move to rename the 'Copenhagen Criteria' the 'Ankara Criteria'. In so doing, the AKP argued that Turkey must consolidate its democracy along European lines, regardless of whether Europeans themselves prove capable of rising to their own standards by delivering membership upon Turkey's eventual fulfilment of the criteria for accession.

Another field in which the democratization discourse is salient is the debate over the permissibility of veiling in public institutions like universities. Pro-religious opponents of the ban often invoke liberal principles such as the right to freedom of expression and religion, the right to access to education, and the right to freedom from discrimination (insofar as religious men face no comparable constraint on university attendance). In this vein, Erdoğan regularly recalls the civil rights movement in the United States to argue that the ban constitutes a violation of the civic rights of religious women. Women affiliated with the AKP, like Hayrünissa Gül, wife of the current president, and Leyla Şahin, a medical student expelled in her fifth year of university for refusing to remove her headscarf during an exam, have also employed liberal arguments in their cases at the European Court of Human Rights.[2] The Court, however, has never found in favour of a Turkish Muslim plaintiff's challenge to secularist institutions. This, in turn, has spurred some within the pro-religious coalition to dismiss the attempts of others within the camp to integrate European-cum-universal and Muslim codes of conduct (a syncretic project which will be explored in more detail in the subsequent section).

Pro-secular anxiety about the headscarf is symptomatic of a broader concern about *mahalle baskısı*—a situation in which the exercise of formal freedoms is inhibited by social pressure. To assuage such fears, AKP figures have self-consciously sought to project an inclusive message. Notable instances include Erdoğan's victory speech after the 2007 elections in which the steep jump in party votes may have reflected the endorsement of non-core constituents impressed by the EU-oriented reform agenda of that period. His post-referendum speech was a watered-down version of the same material. Other examples include extensive outreach to vulnerable groups, which began with an 'opening' to Kurds in the early summer of 2009. This was followed by engagement of Alevis, Armenians, non-Muslims more broadly (e.g. the Jewish and tiny Greek communities), Roma and the liberal intelligentsia. On each occasion, the AKP announced its openness to dialogue and met with community leaders and other commentators for brainstorming sessions.

However, the perlocutionary effects of the AKP democratization discourse, that is, audience receptivity, has been mixed. The democratic openings, for example, gave rise to lively debates in the print and television media which yielded proposals on a wide range of once taboo topics from the reinstatement of Kurdish names for predominantly Kurdish villages, exemption from obligatory religion class for Alevi secondary school students, and reopening of the Greek orthodox seminary in Heybeli/Halki island. Limited follow-up has been defended by pro-AKP pundits on the grounds that merely brokering such questions contributed to the overall desecuritization of public perceptions of these issue areas.

However, critics from these groups as well as from the pro-secular camp more broadly argue that apparent inclusivity is a ploy for votes and that the AKP takes to heart only the well-being of its core conservative constituents. As evidence, they point to moves like the abandonment of promised constitutional reform in the wake of the 2007 elections in favour of a 'quick fix' to the headscarf ban through the passage by passing an *ad hoc* constitutional amendment.[3] AKP proposals in the context of debates over constitutional reform have also been criticized for speaking to partisan interests and not the need for a better system of checks and balances. Unwillingness to lower the 10 per cent electoral threshold which permits the AKP to occupy a disproportionate number of parliamentary seats and keeps smaller parties (e.g. Kurdish parties) out of parliament has also been noted, not least by EU observers who likewise express concern over the Government's increasingly problematic record on press freedom. Last but not least, the AKP has proven unable to assure those who fear not an Iranian-style Islamic revolution but the gradual Islamicization of society. As Binnaz Toprak (2010), an expert on political Islam who has been characterized as the quintessential 'worried modern' (*endişeli modern*) recently wrote:

The source of my worries is not 'fear of a Shari'a state.' I am worried because I find the transformation of democracy into majoritarian populism and tyranny, the otherization of those who are in the minority, and, above all, the presenting of all of this under the name of democratization tremendously problematic.

The (Post-)Islamist Story

Toprak's concern flags the fact that the liberal democratic narrative is often deployed in parallel with a discourse I term (post-)Islamist. The sources of this story go back as far as the late Ottoman period when Islamists, westernists and Turkists touted rival visions of the most appropriate pathway to engaging (and thereby paradoxically resisting) encroaching European powers. A strategy frequently proposed by Islamists was syncretism, namely adoption of western science and technology, and, if need be, western forms of governance which could be reconciled with Islamic frames of reference, while preserving Ottoman-Islamic religiosity. However, when the empire finally collapsed, it was a westernist vision—coupled with a non-irredentist Turkism—which prevailed. It aimed to make a clean break with the pluralistic, religious, and imperial Ottoman-Islamic past in order to reconstitute Turkey as a unitary secular nation-state (Fisher Onar, 2009a). For many of religious persuasion the disestablishment of and attempt to subordinate Islam and negate Ottoman legacies which this entailed was deeply traumatic.

Many such groups mobilized under the mantle of Necmettin Erbakan's National View (MG) movement with the flourishing of multi-party politics. A succession of MG-affiliated political Islamist parties asserted, like their counterparts in Iran, that Muslims who succumbed to the lure of western models would find themselves under the yoke of economic and political, but also social and cultural domination by an exploitative West epitomized in the nefarious image of the Freemason, the Communist and the Zionist. Yet like their antecedents during the Ottoman period, few argued for a rejection of western science, technology, industry or capitalism, calling instead for embrace of western knowledge to empower Muslims in the face of western hegemony. They also employed Islamic idiom to frame promises of social justice and redistribution to rural and urban discontents. This went hand-in-hand with concern for the Muslim 'wretched of the earth' who would come to be epitomized by Bosnians, Chechens, Kosovars and, above all, Palestinians to whom the MG felt a paternalistic sense of responsibility given its will to revitalize Ottoman-Islamic frames of reference. Successful grassroots mobilization eventually permitted MG parties to control municipalities across the country and, by the mid-1990s, a coalition government. Yet, insistence on an anti-westernist and anti-secularist platform ensured the closure of MG parties by the secularist establishment until moderates broke away to form an AKP bent on situating itself within the centre-right tradition—long the goose that lays the golden egg of Turkey's electoral politics.

These two sets of shared meanings—the sense of rupture and transcendental loss at the time of transition from empire to nation-state and the MG tradition—furnish the building blocks of the (post-)Islamist story. Even the party's very name is redolent of this inheritance insofar as the notion of 'justice' in the Islamic canon is comparable to the concept of 'freedom' in liberalism. Similarly, the emphasis on 'development' flags the MG insistence that Muslims must arrive at a level of material well-being that permits them to cast aside a West to whom they are morally superior. The discourse may nonetheless be labelled 'post-Islamist' because AKP religiosity is a far cry from old school attempts to mobilize for the purpose of establishing *Shar'ia* and disengaging from the western-led international system.

Thoroughly reconciled with global capitalism, it is characterized by an ability to 'blend into modern urban spaces, use global communication networks, engage in public debates, follow consumption patterns, learn market rules, enter into secular time, and get acquainted with values of individuation, professionalism, and consumerism, and reflect upon their new practices' (Göle, 2002, p. 174). As such, hardline Islamist allergy to liberal political principles is mitigated or can co-exist with other strands in the AKP repertoire such as the democratization, Ottomanist or Turkey Inc. stories depending on context and audience.

A further dimension of the (post-)Islamist narrative is the use of 'civilization' as the prime unit of analysis. Building on Aydın (2006), the civilizationalist perspective can be conceived of in at least three variants—a binary, an Occidentalist and a syncretic version. The first inverses the Huntingtonian dichotomy to privilege a monolithic Islamic world—of which Turkey is deemed the natural leader—over the West. This reading appeals to many within the AKP rank and file as well as leading figures with roots in the nationalist far-right. It also reflects views espoused earlier in their careers by Erdoğan and President Abdullah Gül to the effect that secularism and Europe are incompatible with Turkey and Islam, stances which they later renounced. A second and more sophisticated form of (post-)Islamist civilizationalism may be termed 'Occidentalist' and is echoed in non-Islamic post-colonial critiques of western modernity. In its (post-)Islamist rendition, Occidentalist civilizationalism anticipates that disillusionment with the excesses of western instrumental reason will push those in search of redemption into the bosom of a restorative Islam. A third approach is syncretic and in keeping with the attempts of pious pundits since the late Ottoman era to embed in Islamic idiom western ideas and practices deemed useful in a Muslim context. It is this logic at work in arguments for the Islamic headscarf which mixes liberal and religious rationales to argue that veiling is at once an individual right and a religious obligation which trumps individual agency. Syncretism also characterizes the engagement of European-cum-universal values in the democratization narratives. Tellingly, Erdoğan explained AKP outreach to the EU to a gathering of conservative nationalists by arguing:

> the achievements of western civilization in technology, culture, democracy, and human rights are irrefutable and universal... all of these things, regardless of who first created them, are our [patrimony]... But we also have values beyond these, values with deep roots shaped by faith and morality... [Turkey is therefore] at the centre of the world's attention because ... it stands to combine the achievements of western modernity with 'authentic' Turco-Muslim values (Erdoğan ile Bahçeli birlik mesajı verdi, 2010, September 10).

This syncretic approach and the notion that Turkey is both intrinsically Islamic and capable of serving as a bridge infuses aspects of domestic and foreign policy. It enables the AKP to downplay Turkish nationalism vis-à-vis Kurds by arguing that legitimate expressions of 'sub-identities' can co-exist with a common 'supra-identity' based on Muslimness rather than Turkishness (Skinner, 2010). The demoting of nationalism also permits receptivity to groups like Turkey's Greek-Orthodox citizens who demand restitution of communal properties confiscated in the context of the Cyprus debacle. At the domestic level then, (post-)Islamist views can be a source of pluralism so long as the aspirations of the groups in question are congruent with the Islamic canon (e.g., the synthesis is not applicable to Turkey's increasingly more vocal lesbian, gay, bi- and trans-sexual [LGBT] community).

As we will see, the idea that Turkey is optimally situated at a 'civilizational focal point' is also at the heart of the vision of Foreign Minister Ahmet Davutoğlu who asserts that the country is willy-nilly a part of the West even if its policy preferences no longer dovetail seamlessly with those of western allies (Bilgin, 2010). Yet, Davutoğlu also argues that Ankara can open channels of communication with isolated and radical actors in regions like the Middle East and seek to resocialize them into the international system, contributing to western as well as Turkey's own regional security.

The perlocutionary impact of this discourse has been mixed at best. Especially when it entails Israel-baiting, the story resonates with the 'Arab street' and domestic publics in advance of elections. But moves like the Turkey–Brazil nuclear deal with Iran and outreach to Hamas arouse ire in Washington and have precipitated a crisis in Turkey–Israeli relations, epitomized by Erdoğan's outburst towards Shimon Peres at Davos in 2009 when he declared: 'You know well how to kill' (Koç, 2011: 384). The tendency to characterize Israel as monolithic and intrinsically violent became more pronounced in the aftermath of the Gaza flotilla killings of nine activists associated with a Turkish NGO, the Humanitarian Relief Foundation (İHH). For the İHH, despite having well-documented and extensive charitable activities, is reputed to have links with militant Islamist organizations and regularly employs unreconstructed Islamist idioms. The AKP denied involvement in the flotilla but made little secret of its sympathy for the organizers and condemned Israel in highly colourful and essentialist language. At the same time, less publicized and more balanced statements were made by many of the same officials. Erdoğan, for one, sought to project the message that he has no bone top pick with Israeli state or society but only with the current right-wing coalition government. High-ranking AKP figures like Arınç, Çelik and Davutoğlu likewise sought on several occasions to frame their criticisms in the language of universal human rights and humanitarianism. Such statements did not differ in substance nor even a great deal in style from the responses of many international organizations like Amnesty International and *Médecins Sans Frontières*. That the inflammatory rather than conciliatory tropes resonated louder in Washington speaks to the explosive impact of mixing metaphors in the face of mixed audiences. It is therefore useful to turn to a third story which encapsulates elements of both the democratization and the (post-)Islamist story, namely the Ottomanist narrative.

The Ottomanist Story

The Ottomanist strand is informed by several of the constituent aspects of the AKP repertoire such as Ottomanist nostalgia and the centre-right/MG will to be a regional leader. Moves to rehabilitate the memory of the Ottoman era were in evidence even during the single party era when pro-religious historians in the 1940s began to challenge the vilification of the Ottomans in early republican historiography (Fisher Onar, 2011b). Ottomanist nostalgia found further expression in MG discourses throughout the 1960s and 1970s and in both nationalist right-wing and centrist platforms by the 1980s and 1990s. By the 2000s, it acquired cross-cutting salience, evident in the newfound passion across Turkish society for Ottoman motifs in the fields of art, design, architecture, fashion, literature, film, and television. At the level of domestic politics too, it has become a rallying cry with festivals celebrating Ottoman milestones like the conquest of Istanbul, and sleek new bank notes upon which Ottoman figures are emblazoned. As noted, Ottoman referents can also be a source of inclusivity towards groups like Kurds or non-Muslims who were part of the Ottoman social fabric but who fared poorly under the rubric of Turkish nationalism.

Similarly, in its foreign policy expression, the Ottomanist story draws on the democratization story and aspects of the (post-)Islamist story to seek the enactment of the democratic peace in a reinvigorated post-Ottoman space. The agenda is set forth in Davutoğlu book *Strategic Depth* (2005) and informed by earlier works steeped in a sophisticated Occidentalism which problematized the exclusive westernist orientation of Turkey's intellectual and policy elites. At the same time, it entails the projection of a message in tune with the EU ethos of mutual recognition in its espousal of the principle of 'zero problems with neighbours' as a policy principle. At the heart of the doctrine is the view that Turkey's historical 'depth'—defined as characteristic of countries located at the epicentre of world historical developments such as Britain, France, Russia, China and Turkey, in tandem with its geostrategic position, gives the country 'strategic depth' with which to pursue intensive diplomatic, economic, and cultural relations in their traditional spheres of influence through bi- and multi-lateral fora.

In operationalizing this agenda, Davutoğlu has been attentive to undesirable perlocutionary effects by customizing historical referents to the interlocutor in question. He has accordingly invoked Turkic and to a lesser extent Muslim brotherhood with Azerbaijani and Central Asians counterparts, and emphasized Muslim fraternity with Arabs and Persians. This testifies to the pragmatic rather than ideological thrust of the project, as does engagement of Ottoman Christian successor states like Serbia and Armenia in which potentially counterproductive Ottomanist references are avoided; indeed, cognizance of its neo-imperial connotations means Davutoğlu renounces the term 'neo-Ottomanist' altogether. While this has only partially assured those who feel it is window-dressing for a post-or bona fide Islamist agenda, others, including some observers in the West, believe Davutoğlu's framework may enable Turkey to harness its true potential (The Economist, 2010b). In this respect, the Ottomanist frame serves a heuristic and branding function for a project I call Turkey Inc. and which may well be the driving force behind AKP activism.

The Turkey Inc. Story

At the beginning of this article I suggested that as much as democratization, (post-)Islamist and Ottomanist discourses are deployed in different and often dizzying combinations for the benefit of diverse audiences, the one constant in AKP positions is the pragmatic pursuit of (soft) power and the attempt to establish Turkey as an energy and trade hub and beacon of prosperity in its regions.

Awareness of Turkey's geostrategic position has informed foreign policy since at least the nineteenth-century 'Eastern Question' when Ottoman diplomats ably exploited the reluctance of European powers to permit another from their ranks to dominate the region. For much of the twentieth century, Turkish policy elites—the military in particular—also cited the country's geostrategic but turbulent location to rationalize massive hard power expenditures (Bilgin, 2007). The geographic pillar of today's 'strategic depth' doctrine likewise envisages Turkey as a pivotal state situated at the crossroads of the Mediterranean, Black and Caspian sea basins and the Balkan, Caucasian and Middle Eastern land basins from which Turkey can project itself into Europe and Africa (Murinson, 2006). In this incarnation of geopolitical reasoning, the aspiration is to soft rather than hard power, evident in the preference for instruments like trade, cultural and educational exchanges, and multilateral platforms. From cultural industries which market soap operas to some 80 million viewers across multiple regions, to a liberal visa regime—and the elimination of visas altogether for the likes of Russian nationals—Turkey power of attraction is growing. The signing of free trade agreements has made Turkey the number one trading partner of smaller states like Georgia as attested to by the assignation of domestic terminal status to Batumi airport (Öniş & Yılmaz, 2009). Aspirations to regional soft power also depend on whether the AKP can turn Turkey into a regional transit hub for gas and petroleum flows between Russia, the Caucasus, Central Asia, Iran, Iraq and Europe.

The bid to foster and profit from overlapping interdependencies could potentially mitigate some of the problematic features of the other strands within the AKP repertoire. It could temper the majoritarian impulse evident in AKP understandings of democratization vis-à-vis cohorts who may well support civilianization of state and society but seek new institutional guarantees for their secular lifestyle. For an AKP that aspires to inspire the Muslim/Arab world, the importance of guaranteeing the rights of 'others' within Turkey's heterogeneous polity should also have been underscored by the courage of peoples from all walks of life in the Arab world—from Islamists and feminists to university students and workers—in their recent uprisings against authoritarian leaders. Similarly, a pragmatic assessment of the costs as well as benefits of populist and ideological appeals to the Muslim 'street' vis-à-vis Israel is necessary if the party is to succeed in becoming a serious broker in the Middle East. The AKP simply has no interest in out-shouting Iran insofar as its own rise is bound up in embeddedness in the global economy (for more on the political economic sources of AKP moderation see Gumuscu, 2010). In this respect, its bid to become a centre of gravity in multiple regions is not served by anti-systemic stands. Last but not least, the Ottomanist story provides a heuristic and normative frame which is satisfying to domestic, regional and international audiences via which to pursue the consolidation of Turkey Inc. It is therefore in the interest of European and American actors to recognize that AKP activism is bound up in its attempt to become a regional (soft) power and engage the party in such a fashion as to encourage moderation and pragmatism.

Conclusion

In this article, I developed an analytical framework informed by the insights of speech act theory and its appropriation by constructivist policy analysts to examine the illocutionary content and intent of AKP discourses and their often unintended and sometimes explosive perlocutionary impact. This enabled me to account for the apparent inconsistencies in AKP discourses. I showed that democratization discourses and EU/universal value references are typically employed in domestic contests with the remnants of the old secularist establishment and vis-à-vis western actors, while (post-)Islamist referents are salient with regard to the Israeli/Palestinian question and aimed at Muslim/Arab audiences and alienating for many in the West. Ottomanist discourses, meanwhile, are used to bolster domestic confidence and relations with diverse regional actors, and have received a mixed reception in the West. I went on to suggest that this framework in fact serves as supra-structural packaging for the material interests that animate the fourth and arguably driving story behind AKP initiatives, namely Turkey Inc. This is the goal of establishing Turkey as a (soft) power—a hub and gateway—for transactions across its multiple regions and hinterlands. The pragmatic thrust of this project may help mitigate the tensions embedded in and across the other stories within the AKP repertoire, providing a platform for positive-sum co-operation with western allies. This argument could be corroborated by further research which systematically traces the political economic considerations that inform illocutionary acts. Such research would also speak to the growing interest in reintegrating foreign policy analysis into the broader discipline of IR by anchoring it to a constructivism steeped in a subjectivist ontology which is nevertheless compatible with interpretivist (discourse analytic) but also positivist (political economic) epistemologies.

Notes

[1] Speech delivered at Examination Schools in Oxford in October 2004.
[2] Gül withdrew her petition against the Turkish state when the AKP came to power.
[3] The amendment was later overturned by the Constitutional Court.

References

Aydın, C. (2006) Between Occidentalism and the global Left: Islamist critiques of the West in Turkey, *Comparative Studies of South Asia, Africa and the Middle East*, 26(3): 446–461.
Bilgin, P. (2007) 'Only strong states can survive in Turkey's geography': the uses of 'geopolitical truths' in Turkey, *Political Geography*, 26(7): 740–745.
(2007, September 10) Erdoğan ile Bahçeli birlik mesajı verdi, *Milliyet* cited in Fisher Onar, N. (2009c, November) A righteous civilization: Turkish elite perceptions of European universalism. Unpublished doctoral thesis, University of Oxford.
(2010, July 11) Davutoğlu: Batı'nın parçasıyız, *Zaman*. Available at: http://www.zaman.com.tr/haber.do?haber no=1004439 (accessed 10 March 2011).
Davutoğlu, A. (2005) Stratejik Derinliği (Istanbul: Küre Yayınları).
Economist (2010a, October 23) Doing it by the book, *Economist*. Available at: http://www.economist.com/node/17276384 (accessed 10 March 2011).
Economist (2010b, October 23) Is Turkey turning it back on the West? *Economist*. Available at: http://www.economist.com/node/17309065 (accessed 10 March 2011).
Fisher Onar, N. (2009a) Echoes of a universalism lost: rival representations of the Ottomans in today's Turkey, *Middle Eastern Studies*, 45(2), 229–241.
Fisher Onar, N. (2009b) *Neo-Ottomanism, Historical Legacies, and Turkish Foreign Policy*, EDAM/German Marshall Fund Working Paper Series, 2009/3. Available online at: http://www.edam.org.tr/index.php?option=com_content&task=view&id=211&Itemid=33 (accessed 11 March 2011).
Fisher Onar, N. (2011a) Democratic depth: the missing ingredient in Turkey's domestic/foreign policy nexus? in: O. Anastasakis, A. Kadıoğlu, M. Karlı & K. Öktem (Eds) *Turkish Foreign Policy in a Changing World* (Istanbul: Bilgi UP).
Fisher Onar, N. (2011b) Continuity or rupture? The historiography of the Ottoman past and its political uses, in: K. Nicolaidis & B. Sebe (Eds) *Echoes of Colonialism* (Cambridge: Cambridge UP).
Göle, N. (2002) Islam in public: new visibilities and new imaginaries, *Public Culture*, 14(1), 173–190.
Gumuscu, S. (2010) Class, status, and party: the changing face of political Islam in Turkey and Egypt, *Comparative Political Studies*, 43(7), 835–861.
Koç, M. B. (2011) Reflections on the Davos crisis in the Turkish Press and the views of opinion leaders of the Turkish Jews on the crisis. *Turkish Studies*, 12(3).
Murinson, A. (2006) The strategic depth of Turkish foreign policy, *Middle Eastern Studies*, 42(6), 945–964.
Öniş, Z. & Yılmaz, S. (2009) Between Europeanization and Euro-Asianism: foreign policy activism in Turkey during the AKP era, *Turkish Studies*, 10(1), 7–24.
Skinner, Q. (2002) *Visions of Politics* (Cambridge: Cambridge UP).
(2005, November 24) Üst kimlik' tartışması, *ntvmsnbc*, Available online at: http://www.ntvmsnbc.com/news/350771.asp (accessed 11 March 2011).
Toprak, B. (2010, October 17) Neden endişeliyim?, *Radikal*. Available at: http://www.radikal.com.tr/Default.aspx?aType=RadikalYazar&ArticleID=1024040&Yazar=B%DDNNAZ%20TOPRAK&Date=17.10.2010&CategoryID=97. (accessed March 7, 2010).

Ombudsmanship and Turkey's Europeanization in 'World Society'

DIDEM BUHARI-GULMEZ*
Royal Holloway, University of London

ABSTRACT   *This article investigates Europeanization in a candidate country from a macro-sociological perspective. From the point of view of sociology, extant Europeanization studies treat culture only in a reductionist manner. In particular, 'sender-receiver' models overlook the domestic perceptions that translate, vernacularize or reframe exogenous conditionality. Furthermore, 'goodness of fit' approaches 'bringing domestic agency back in' misleadingly reinforce the image that the domestic and the external spheres are easily separated. By studying the ombudsmanship reform in Turkey, the article concludes that: (1) the content of Europeanization is not purely European; (2) the role for domestic norm entrepreneurs in leading cultural change is variable and constrained; and (3) domestic motivations for Europeanization include exogenous factors trespassing upon EU conditionality, that is, global culture/world society.*

Introduction

From a macro-sociological perspective led by the Stanford School on sociological neo-institutionalism (Meyer *et al.*, 1997; see also Drori & Krücken, 2009; Buhari-Gulmez, 2010; Boli, Gallo-Cruz and Mathias 2010), extant Europeanization studies overlook the constructed nature of EU agency, restrict their focus to socialization and norm entrepreneurship and finally have a limited grasp of domestic reactions towards EU-led reforms. By studying the reform on ombudsmanship in Turkey, an EU candidate country, this article suggests going beyond the 'sender–receiver' and 'goodness of fit' studies in order to locate the missing link between Europeanization and globalization. The research findings are based on a web survey the author conducted between January and April 2010 with 261 'EU/external affairs' experts in Turkey and on follow-up face-to-face interviews conducted between October and December 2010 with sixteen Turkish parliamentarians[1] (including nine parliamentarians from the Government) who were leading members of the parliamentary committees on External Relations and EU Harmonization of the 23rd term of Turkish Parliament (from 2007 to 2011) as well as three (anonymous) bureaucrats from two different Turkish Ministries, Serkan Çatalpınar (head of the EU section in Ankara Bar Association), Hatice Yazgan (academic affiliated with the EU research centre ATAUM in Ankara University) and Mustafa Durna (founding leader of the

Non-Governmental Organization 'Turkey Association of Committees for Monitoring Parliament and Elected Officials' TUMIKOM).

First, the article reviews the extant Europeanization scholarship under two main headings: 'sender–receiver' models and 'goodness of fit' studies. Second, it advances sociological insights highlighting three major weaknesses of the Europeanization literature: (1) rationalistic ontology of EU agency; (2) overemphasis on socialization mechanisms; and (3) a limited understanding of domestic reactions to EU-led reforms. The final section introduces the reform of ombudsmanship in Turkey as a case-study.

'EU Matters'

Europeanization implies that EU conditionality explains domestic change in member and candidate countries. In the extant literature, Europeanization is used to explain policy change, administrative innovation, cultural change and new identity formation, which renders the term ambiguous, if not meaningless (Howell, 2004). During the Eastern Enlargement, the transition of many ex-communist countries to liberal economy and democracy were presented as successful cases of Europeanization (Schimmelfennig & Sedelmeier, 2005, p. 3). There are two major tendencies in studies on Europeanization dealing with candidate countries. First, 'sender–receiver' models treat Europeanization as a top–down and unidirectional process in which the domestic arena is merely a passive receiver of policies determined at the EU level. Accordingly, Europeanization is relegated to processes of policy transfer (Howell, 2004). Hence, the nature (direct/indirect) and strength (hard/soft) of the EU-level stimuli determine the likeliness of domestic reform. Domestic change is more likely when the EU acts on the basis of treaty competences and legislative directives/hard law whereas reform is less likely in sectors where the EU rules are non-enforceable/soft law (Featherstone & Papadimitriou, 2008, p. 4). Moreover, positive integration directly addresses the institutional system at the national level; negative integration redistributes power and alters domestic actor constellations; and 'framing' integration transforms domestic beliefs and expectations (Knill & Lehmkuhl, 1999). Briefly, the EU's differentiated impact on the domestic arena results from the EU's own structure.

'Sender–receiver' models are criticized for overlooking domestic agency (Howell, 2004, p. 3). States do not passively 'download' EU policies. Rather, 'ideas and pressures flow in both directions' (Featherstone & Papadimitriou, 2008, p. 1). Policy makers at national and European arenas are interdependent through 'vertical and horizontal networks and institutional linkages' (Featherstone & Kazamias, 2001, p. 1). From this critical perspective, Europeanization depends on the 'goodness of fit' between EU conditionality and domestic resources, capabilities, culture and institutions (Börzel & Risse, 2000). 'Goodness of fit' models of Europeanization confirm that '[d]iffusion processes are unlikely to produce perfect cloning of the prescriptions offered. What is diffused is likely to be transformed during the process of diffusion' (Olsen, 2002, p. 938). Hence, they emphasize the processes through which EU stimuli are received, translated and transformed before being adopted or rejected.

The 'goodness of fit' studies refine 'sender–receiver' models in terms of rejecting top–down and unidirectional accounts of Europeanization and taking domestic agency more seriously. However, 'goodness of fit' studies assume that domestic and European spheres could analytically be separated and emphasize EU agency. Hence, they overlook the fact that the EU is embedded in a larger cultural environment which constitutes its agency and thus, what the EU diffuses is not purely European. Furthermore, the agency of norm entrepreneurs is contestable. The success of the norm entrepreneurship in encouraging reforms by claiming a 'fit' between exogenous norms and domestic culture varies significantly. Finally, domestic attitudes towards EU conditionality are largely driven by global culture rather than nationalist cost-effective logic.

Macro-Sociological Insights

The Europeanness of the norms propagated by the EU is generally taken for granted although the latter owe much to the United Nations and global processes like liberalization. Furthermore, domestic compliance is not necessarily associated with EU conditionality. While many non-EU countries follow similar norms in the absence of EU pressures, certain EU members deviate from them. So, 'it is difficult to say who is and who is not European' (Meyer, 2001, p. 10). Yet, the EU is often depicted as a socializing agent paradoxically immune from external socialization pressures, *as if it operates in a void*. It thus seems to be devoid of a larger social context that gives meaning to its identity, norms and interests.

The Stanford School on sociological institutionalism alternatively argues that agency is not autonomous but 'constructed, scripted, legitimated' by the wider cultural system (Meyer & Jepperson, 2000, pp. 101–103). Accordingly, states with different resources and institutional arrangements adopt similar policies because they follow 'world cultural models' that provide them scripts for appropriate behaviour and norms (Meyer, 2009, p. 19). Thus, the global spread of standards on human rights, education, science and environment are seen as the products of world cultural scripts rather than conditionality (Soysal, 1994; Bradley & Ramirez, 1996; Meyer *et al.*, 1997; Schofer, 2003). In sum, as the analytical boundaries between domestic and international become blurred, national decisions involve the recognition of global standards (Ramirez, 1987, p. 327).

Although many global norms can be traced back to European countries, they no longer belong to Europe. If the European/western origins are highlighted, they are perceived as hegemonic (see Cortell & Davis, 2000, p. 74). For instance, the idea of democracy cherished in the EU membership criteria is historically derived from Greece but the EU abstains from suggesting a purely Greek prototype. It rather advances a global blueprint that is flexible enough to allow for cultural and national variations.

In this context, Europeanization studies stressing socialization, learning and norm diffusion ignore the fact that these processes often produce limited exchange of strategic information rather than cultural/cognitive change (Strang & Meyer, 1993). Instead of particular norms, 'assemblages' (Levitt, 2010) of ideas, objects and norms matter by gaining a diffuse cultural authority. A norm is never a stand-alone idea. It is always contextualized within a set of norms, ideas, objects and scripts that are generally accepted as 'common sense' and promoted by international organizations, states, scientific communities and individuals. This implies an emergent world society, which is not a world hegemon but is rather 'a seamless unity' in terms of providing universalistic images and definitions of social life.

Therefore, contemporary social movements stem from large-scale cultural processes, which diffuse across societies by creating 'magnetic spheres' that attract and assemble objects, ideas and people together. Incompatible ideas, norms and organizations are transformed in line with the prevailing world trends. Thus, cultural diffusion is mainly based on theorization rather than concrete social exchanges (Strang & Meyer, 1993).

'Every social behaviour is both an action within a frame and a theory of the frame itself' (Meyer, 1981, p. 898). Accordingly, a reform is adopted when it resonates with the prevailing 'assemblages' in world culture, and the adoption of the norm in turn empowers the existing world culture. Consequently, social institutions and norms spread in dissimilar countries which have no social contact with each other. It is thus necessary to reject the idea that domestic culture is stable, homogenous and maintains clear boundaries against the external world. The domestic sphere is rather culturally divided (Boyle, 2002). Moreover, exogenous norms are not purely foreign. They mostly have a flexible nature, which allows for cultural variations. Consequently, an analytical separation of the domestic from the external is implausible.

Another related limitation in Europeanization studies is the overemphasis on norm entrepreneurs or 'change agents' who seek to render exogenous norms more acceptable in the domestic arena (Finnemore & Sikkink, 1998; Börzel & Risse, 2000). Internal divisions within the domestic culture make norm entrepreneurship a difficult task. Strategies that overlook the heterogeneity of domestic society fail to expand reformist segments. Finally, Europeanization scholars limit their focus to national and European levels while studying the EU effect on a candidate state. Yet, Europeanization is often instrumentalized by national governments aiming at overall modernization and liberalization (Featherstone & Papadimitriou, 2008, p. 28). For instance, Greek elites used the EU agenda to advance the privatization of national airlines (Featherstone & Papadimitriou, 2008, p. 30). Hence, global cultural processes inform domestic responses to the EU membership process. Accordingly, the content of Europeanization is not necessarily European and domestic reactions to EU conditionality involve trans-European issues. The following section explains that an institution diffused by the EU, ombudsmanship, derives from Europe but it is embraced as a universalistic model.

The Europeanization literature looks at the reform on national ombudsmanship only superficially. Occasionally, the establishment of ombudsmanship is mentioned briefly as an example of the EU's empowering impact on domestic civil society (Stavridis, 2003, p. 35). However, there is a tendency to overlook domestic perceptions and explain government's refusal to establish ombudsmanship with power politics. For instance, the Czech government blocked the reform on ombudsmanship claiming that it would weaken its authority (Pehe, 1996, p. 37). This article aims to study the establishment of the Turkish ombudsman from a macro-sociological perspective, which takes individual perceptions into account and transcends the mainstream interest-based approaches.

Ombudsmanship as a Global Script: The Turkish Case

The ombudsman, meaning 'representative' in Swedish, deals with public complaints against administrative neglect, abuse or malpractice (Gregory & Giddings, 2002, p. 7). Originating from Sweden in the eighteenth century, it was spread globally in two major waves. In the 1960s, it spread as a problem-solving mechanism vis-à-vis increasing governmental complexity in liberal democratic countries (Gregory & Giddings, 2002, p. 9). Since the 1980s, more than 120 countries dissimilar in terms of political culture, geographical location and economic development, have established an ombudsman system (Sezen, 2001, p. 73). However, there are significant national variations in terms of the powers, status, duties, appointment and working procedures of ombudsmanship (Al-Wahab, 1979, p. 150). For instance in France, the primary duty of an ombudsman is mediation whereas in Spain, it is known as the 'protector of human rights'. Nevertheless, there is sufficient cognitive consensus on its basic meaning. Ombudsmanship is about 'upholding the dignity of the individual and his basic rights' (Al-Wahab, 1979, p. 150).

Unlike the 1960s when it was seen as a problem-solving mechanism for liberal democracies, ombudsmanship today has become a 'logo of modern democracies' (Al-Wahab, 1979, p. 140). Such cognitive shift owes much to the UN, which promoted ombudsmanship as part of its human rights programme (Al-Wahab, 1979, p. 138). Besides, both European and non-European academics, and experts expanded the idea of ombudsmanship (Gregory & Giddings, 2002, p. 20). Overall, although ombudsmanship originated in Europe, its rapid spread around the world implies that it has become a universalistic institution, embedded in the world cultural processes of individualization and human rights. It is universalistic in the sense that it claims to be applicable everywhere and to be of benefit to everybody (Lechner & Boli, 2005, p. 44). A 'universalistic' nature implies flexibility. It allows for adjustments in line with national, local or individual particularities.

The reform of Turkish ombudsmanship is an important but understudied case. The case study shows that explaining domestic reform with EU conditionality is misleading. First, the temporal order falsifies the primacy of EU-level stimuli because Turkish discussions on reforms had already started before the institutionalization of the Copenhagen criteria at the EU level. Second, domestic compliance is not necessarily associated with the EU's adaptational pressures. In some sectors—like ombudsmanship—where EU pressures are relatively lower, domestic support for reform in Turkey is stronger than that in other sectors—like free movement of capital—where the EU conditionality is strict. Therefore, domestic motivations for reform need further investigation. The article suggests that for Turkish reformists, the necessity to comply with world standards comes before EU conditionality. Furthermore, there is a reluctance to adopt a European blueprint without certain adjustments in Turkey. David Phillips (2009) explains that:

> Actually, what were the Copenhagen criteria have now become the Ankara criteria. The reform agenda has been adopted by the government. The government is working on democratic reforms not to satisfy the demands of the EU or the US but because of its own interests. And that is exactly the way it should be. It is a democratic project, which is conceived of and prosecuted by the government of Turkey on behalf of the Turkish people.

Hence, 'Ankara criteria' is advanced as a nationalized version of EU conditionality by leading politicians, academics and opinion leaders in Turkey. Therefore, the Europeanness of the EU-led reforms is de-emphasized. However, research shows only mixed results in efforts to reframe EU-led reforms like ombudsmanship as part and parcel of the national culture. The efforts of Turkish norm entrepreneurs to present ombudsmanship as an element of the Ottoman past and Islamic culture of Turkish society seem to have failed so far. The most successful norm entrepreneurship strategy has been 'mirroring' the UN's approach, that is, linking ombudsmanship with the consolidation of democracy and human rights in Turkey.

The reform on ombudsmanship involves an iterative process in Turkey. Although postponed by the 1980 coup d'état, official undertakings for ombudsmanship started in the 1970s. In 1991, the official 'Research on Public Administration' suggested the expansion of an existing institution, the State Supervisory Council, towards fulfilling the functions of ombudsmanship (Sezen, 2001, p. 85). However, the State Supervisory Council was officially dependent upon the Presidency of the Turkish Republic. So, the suggestion was rejected by the Government of the time as inappropriate. In the late 1990s, civil society actors including the Turkish Industrialists and Businessmen's Association (TÜSİAD), the Union of Chambers and Commodity Exchanges of Turkey (TOBB) and HAK-İŞ Trade Union Confederation called for a Turkish ombudsman (Avşar, 1999). Similarly, the seventh and eighth Development Plans issued by the State Planning Organization recommended that Turkey should follow the example of European countries which had already adopted ombudsmanship. Finally, a law on ombudsmanship was referred to the Turkish Parliament in October 2000. However, it was not voted on until 2006 because Turkish parliamentarians were highly divided over the issue (Hekimoğlu, 2000).

Furthermore, exogenous pressures on the Turkish government increased following Turkey's official candidacy for EU membership in 1999. The EU encouraged Turkey to collaborate with European countries to facilitate the establishment of Turkish ombudsmanship. Thus, Turkey accepted the joint proposal by Greece and Austria and in October 2004, they co-organized an EU-funded conference on ombudsmanship. Under both domestic and external pressures, the Turkish Parliament adopted the law on ombudsmanship on 28 September 2006 (law no. 5548). Yet, both the Turkish President and 123 parliamentarians from the main opposition party asked immediately for the annulment of the law claiming that it was incompatible with the constitutional principle of separation of powers. Two years later, the Turkish Constitutional Court unanimously ruled against a Turkish ombudsman on the grounds that it would violate the constitutional provisions on the integrity of the administration and the Parliamentary duties (Court decision no. E. 2006/140, K. 2008/15, dated 25 December 2008, appeared in *Official Gazette* on 4 April 2009). The annulment of the law cancelled Turkish–Greek–Austrian collaboration on ombudsmanship. It also attracted much criticism. A Turkish legal scholar, Ergun Özbudun (2009) criticized the Constitutional Court for ignoring the very essence of ombudsmanship: its autonomy. Besides, external pressures ensued. The Human Rights Commissioner of the Council of Europe stressed the urgent need for a Turkish ombudsman. Moreover, International NGOs including Transparency International and Freedom House regularly report that socio-political liberties are still problematic in Turkey. Under such pressures, Turkish Parliament adopted the legislation on 'Kamu Denetçiliği' (ombudsmanship) with 334 'yes', seventy rejections and two abstentions on 22 April 2010. A referendum on 12 September 2010 confirmed several constitutional amendments, including the establishment of a Turkish ombudsman.

The parliamentary debates in both 2006 and 2010 as well as the interviews conducted by the author with sixteen Turkish parliamentarians, show that there is a sufficient cognitive consensus on the definition of ombudsmanship. Both government and opposition members emphasize that ombudsmanship, established worldwide, contributes to the culture of human rights, democracy and citizen-centred governance. Those who oppose the reform explain that they are not against the institution itself but to its manipulation by the Government. For instance, during the plenary session on 15 June 2006, İzzet Çetin from the main opposition party, Republican People's Party (CHP), argued that he was uncertain about the real motive behind the reform. He questioned whether the Turkish ombudsman would be 'window-dressing' for Turkey's commitment to European norms. Similarly, during the plenary session on 22 April 2010 opposition MPs contested the constitutional amendments including the reform on ombudsmanship. Akın Birdal from the pro-Kurdish Peace and Democracy Party (BDP) asked why the Government waited so long for such reform and asserted that the real motive behind the amendments might be the Government's desire to please the EU in order to receive greater EU funds. Furthermore, Behiç Çelik from the right wing Nationalist Action Party (MHP) argued that the reform was neither sufficiently debated in the public sphere nor adapted to Turkey's specific conditions. Engin Altay (CHP) stated that in semi-democracies like Turkey, the ombudsman could never work independently. Similarly, Nevin Gaye Erbatur (CHP) stressed the need to guarantee the ombudsman's impartiality and autonomy.

In general, the idea of ombudsmanship finds strong support among Turkish parliamentarians. Both government and opposition members highlight the link between ombudsmanship and democratization. However, their cultural strategies—for making ombudsmanship more acceptable in Turkey—vary. Opposition members tend to highlight the necessity to harmonize with the EU whereas government MPs claim that ombudsmanship is inspired by the Ottoman/Islamic culture, and its adoption would 'reconcile Turkey with its own past' (Alaattin Büyükkaya, plenary session in Turkish Parliament on 15 June 2006). For instance, during the plenary session on 15 June 2006, Algan Hacaloğlu (CHP) first emphasized the function of ombudsmanship in consolidating human rights and democracy in Turkey, then added that the reform was part of the EU conditionality and Turkey should take the EU ombudsman as a model. From a different perspective, Alaattin Büyükkaya from the governing party AKP (Justice and Development Party) argued that the law on ombudsmanship was a direct attempt to consolidate modern citizen-centred governance. He then continued to say that it was the Ottoman Empire which first established such a system before it was successfully implemented by the West.

Interview findings show a similar trend. All of the AKP members emphasized the Ottoman/Islamic/domestic origins of ombudsmanship. Yaşar Yakış, ex-minister of foreign affairs and the current Chair of the Parliamentary Committee on Turkey's Harmonization with the EU, explains that the main reason behind his personal support for ombudsmanship is the Ottoman origins of the institution. Taha Aksoy argues that the Ottomans who successfully governed multiple nations as a union could be a role-model for the EU. The 'kadı' (religious judge) system is often mentioned as the source of ombudsmanship. Yet, there are also other similar institutions such as 'Divan-ı Mezalim' and 'Muhtesip' whose duty was to receive public complaints against the officials of the Ottoman Sultan (Şafaklı, 2009). Such strategy of linking ombudsmanship with Ottoman/Islamic culture finds support in EU ranks too. After his meeting with Egemen Bağış—Chief Negotiator for Turkey's accession to the EU—on 28 January 2011 in Brussels, the European ombudsman, Nikiforos Diamandouros announced to the Turkish press that 'the idea of an ombudsman has its origins in the Ottoman Empire and now it will get back to you [Turks] this time [via a different route]' (Milliyet, 2011).

Nevertheless, opposition MPs tend to contest such historical links. For instance, Canan Arıtman, Algan Hacaloğlu, Atilla Kart and Hüseyin Pazarcı from CHP argue that it is irrational to compare two different time periods. Hacaloğlu explains that the 'kadı' system which functioned in a different historical context could not be a model for ombudsmanship. Pazarcı suggests that the Ottoman Empire implied complete obedience to the Sultan, which is very different from today's liberal democratic world. Accordingly, 'although one can find similarities in the mechanisms that deal with public complaints in the past and present, the "spirit" is essentially different' (Pazarcı, interview 2010).

Similarly, Ufuk Uras (BDP) argues that comparing Ottoman society that was based on communities (cemaat) with individual-oriented European societies is far-fetched: 'One needs to beware such comparisons; even Turkey of the twenty-first century is incomparable with Turkey of the twentieth century' (Uras, interview 2010). Additionally, Hatice Yazgan (academic) suspiciously asks why the so-called Ottoman tradition of ombudsmanship had ceased to exist in modern Turkey. An anonymous bureaucrat and Serkan Çatalpınar (lawyer) argue that ombudsmanship is incompatible with Turkish culture because the understanding of compromise and democracy is still developing in the country. According to Mustafa Durna (NGO leader), 'we always have "laws *a la Turca*"', which implies that the Parliament passed the law on ombudsmanship without determining the working procedures for the Turkish ombudsman. Finally, a bureaucrat concludes that 'there is no rational reason to establish a national ombudsman in Turkey' (interview 2010).

The survey[2] findings examined the opinions of EU/foreign affairs experts in Turkey because they 'filter' external messages before transmitting them to both policy makers and the domestic public. Hence, the survey asked them 'Do you agree that ombudsmanship should be established in Turkey?' Respondents were free to give more than one answer. Therefore, the total sum of answers exceeds 100 per cent. The findings show that the majority (66 per cent) of the Turkish experts support ombudsmanship because 'ombudsmanship is a global institution and it is an important condition for being counted as a modern and democratic country'. Only 20.7 per cent emphasize that it is an EU precondition for Turkey's membership. According to 12.6 per cent, 'the establishment of ombudsmanship in Turkey would demonstrate Turkey's Europeanness'. Other responses include: 'The institution of ombudsmanship is still absent in many countries of the world. So, it is not perceived as a beneficial institution in the world' (10 per cent); 'Ombudsmanship is against national interests' (10.7 per cent); and 'Ombudsmanship is against national identity' (3.4 per cent). The question also allowed for constitutive answers by providing an 'Other' category.

The emphasis upon the world-level variables is as high as 76 per cent. Hence, informants follow the developments in the world before determining their attitude. While 66 per cent find ombudsmanship as a legitimate global institution, 10 per cent stress its variable presence in the globe from a rationalist perspective. The emphasis on the European-level variables is limited to 33.3 per cent. While 20.7 per cent of the experts suggest complying with the EU in rationalistic terms, 12.6 per cent highlight the necessity to comply with European culture. National-level variables seem to gather the least support (14.1 per cent). According to 10.7 per cent, the reform is unnecessary and 3.4 per cent stress a cultural mismatch. Nevertheless, constitutive answers explicitly reinforce national-level factors and close the gap between the emphasis upon the European and the national-level factors without affecting the predominance of the world-level factors. For instance, an NGO activist argues that the costs and benefits of ombudsmanship vary across societies and thus, 'one-size-fits-all' accounts of ombudsmanship should be rejected. A bureaucrat defends the idea that even though ombudsmanship seems useful in theory, its application might produce adverse effects. Twelve informants state that the institution needs to be adjusted to Turkey's specific conditions, including multi-ethnicity, large population and its domestic political culture with high levels of corruption and ideological conflicts in state institutions. A lawyer comments, 'we should establish ombudsmanship not to prove something to the EU but because it is beneficial to ourselves'. Similarly, a public servant adds that regardless of the policies in Europe or elsewhere, Turkey should establish ombudsmanship because the latter consolidates the culture of equity and human rights in a country.

The interview findings are similar. When asked whether they would support ombudsmanship without any EU pressure, interviewees confirm that the absence of EU conditionality would not change their firm belief in the institution. Ufuk Uras (BDP) explains that he was already a staunch supporter of ombudsmanship while he was an undergraduate student (interview 2010). Ahmet Kenan Tanrıkulu (MHP) argues that calls for reforms were already there even before the EU conditionality on Turkey included ombudsmanship. So, 'it is not meaningful to identify the reform with the EU' (Tanrıkulu, interview 2010). Mehmet Sait Dilek (AKP) explains that 'reforms are made for Turkish people's sake, not for the sake of the EU' (Dilek, interview 2010). Abdullah Çalışkan (AKP) concludes:

> No matter whether you [Turkey] or the EU mentions it [the reform] first, what really matters here is the 'collective mind'. Wherever you go, 'what is right' does not change according to different locales. In such a globalized world, everybody is in interaction with everybody else due to air travel, tourism, internet technologies, etc. We can both learn from and teach the EU. It is inconceivable that Turkey takes/learns everything from Europe. This is a mutual relationship. The EU borrows models from us too. (Çalışkan, interview 2010)

Therefore, the 'EU effect' seems to be variable and constrained. Several informants explicitly state that Turkey should not pursue reform just because the EU asks for it. Rather than the EU conditionality, many informants stress the need to consider national interests and political culture. Such concerns are frequently expressed in other parts of the world too (Mollah & Uddin, 2004). Hence, there is a general interest in refining exogenous norms in line with the domestic specificities. Only one respondent (out of 261) mentioned that ombudsmanship originated in the Ottoman Empire and thus, s/he saw no need for adjustment. However, nine informants explicitly stated that ombudsmanship was incompatible with Turkish culture.

Accordingly, the strategy to reframe ombudsmanship as originating from domestic culture fails to mobilize Turkish experts' support. The strategy fails because it overlooks the domestic cleavages over the Ottoman past and Islamic culture. Some perceive the modern Turkish Republic as the antithesis of the Ottoman Empire and others are ultra-sensitive about keeping religious notions separate from political life. Hence, when the AKP government claims a historical link between ombudsmanship and the Ottoman/Islamic culture, it fails to gather support from the Kemalist and secularist segments of Turkish society. Moreover, certain neo-Ottomanist and pro-Islamic segments of the society oppose the reform and call for the establishment of a purely Ottoman institution, *muhtesip*. However, the failure of the norm entrepreneurs in convincing Turkish experts about the link between Ottoman/Islamic culture and ombudsmanship does not mean that the reform is opposed in Turkey. On the contrary, an overwhelming majority of the informants express support for the ombudsman system. They support ombudsmanship because it is an element of the modern democratic world. Turkish ombudsman would prove Turkey's compliance with the modern world *as a legitimate actor of world society*.

Concluding Remarks

This article suggests that the effect of the EU's adaptational pressures towards a candidate country is variable and constrained. Domestic accounts for reform falsify 'sender–receiver' models of Europeanization by highlighting the need to refine EU-led norms and institutions in congruence with Turkish people's interests, culture and 'ways of doing things'. In addition, the 'goodness of fit' approaches to Europeanization do not explain why Turkish reformists emphasize the resonance of ombudsmanship with global cultural 'assemblages' such as human rights, democracy and good governance rather than the potential link or 'fit' between ombudsmanship and Turkish culture. Hence, the extant Europeanization studies fail to capture the complexity underlying the domestic arena which is heterogeneous, dynamic and under the strong influence of exogenous cultural flows.

In the context of Turkey's Europeanization, ombudsmanship is supported in Turkey because it is an appropriate and legitimate element of the modern world. Contrary to the common assumptions about the EU's independent role, the EU's adaptational pressures are only reported as secondary and complementary factors in supporting the reform in the domestic arena. Furthermore, the direction of the EU effect is not necessarily clear. While the EU conditionality convinces some to comply with it, it also provokes others to react against it. Many informants de-emphasize the EU effect and claim that the reform responds to Turkey's own interests. In particular, nationalist segments of society react negatively to the association of reforms with EU membership conditionality as they tend to view European pressures as hegemonic over Turkey. Rather than a particular region or country, it is the universalistic arena, that is, world society, which triggers the reform on ombudsmanship. In other words, if the exogenous pressures are culturally universalistic and justified in terms of the prevailing global 'assemblages'—for example, UN or INGO pressures—they tend not to be perceived as hegemonic. They are taken for granted as common sense with which one should naturally comply. It is unthinkable not to comply with them.

Consequently, Turkish actors embrace the reform almost automatically and only afterwards provide post-hoc and rationalized arguments for the adoption of the reform. The Turkish Parliament passed the ombudsmanship bill in 2006 without considering its compatibility with the Turkish Constitution, and adopted the recent law on ombudsmanship before determining the working procedures of the Turkish ombudsman. If the reform was a result of a thought-out process, Turkish legislators would have already determined the ways in which the institution would work efficiently in the Turkish context before passing the law. This shows that reform is not adopted out of efficiency concerns. It rather sought to consolidate Turkey's legitimate actorness in the modern world. In other words, reform reflects a search for external legitimacy rather than nationalist cost-effective logic. However, this does not mean that world society leads automatically to domestic compliance. Sezen (2001, p. 93) criticizes those who see the ombudsman as a 'savior' and embrace it without even thinking of its relevance, content and resonance with Turkish society and culture.

However, norm entrepreneurship centred on Turkey's Ottoman and Islamic past fails to encourage reform. Therefore, rather than diffusion processes where translation and vernacularization take place, it would be more useful to concentrate on the structure of world society because cultural strategies used by norm entrepreneurs mostly fail when there is no link between the reform and the global 'assemblages' in the world society. Yet, world society is paradoxically decoupled as it simultaneously produces such contradictory processes as globalization and localization. Hence, the modern world spreads the idea that modern actors should preserve local and national peculiarities (Robertson (1990) calls this paradox 'glocalization'). Turkish informants thus share a common analytical framework with the rest of the world that encourages the belief that modern actors should stress their uniqueness and autonomy (Boyle & Meyer, 1998).

Finally, a macro-sociological approach to Turkey's Europeanization implies that the EU-led reforms are—almost automatically—embraced by domestic actors when they are universalistic or backed by the world society. De-emphasizing EU conditionality, domestic actors justify their attitude in line with what is 'right' in the context of global culture. Ombudsmanship is supported because it is legitimized by the ideas on human rights, individual freedoms, citizen-centred/good governance and so on. However, this is puzzling because European countries are often perceived as the originators of universalistic models. Therefore, one needs to grasp the co-constitutiveness between Europe and world society. As with all other international organizations, the EU is both 'enactor' and 'carrier' of universalistic models of world society. This does not only establish the missing link between the European and the global, but it also explains why states like Turkey are willing to identify with the EU. Rather than a club, the EU presents an opportunity to adjust more readily to the dynamic world society.

Acknowledgements

I would like to thank Chris Rumford, Seckin Baris Gulmez, an anonymous reviewer and the Association of EU Experts of Turkey.

Notes

[1] (Surname–alphabetical order) Taha Aksoy, Canan Arıtman, Mehmet Ceylan (vice-chair, External Relations Committee), Abdullah Çalışkan, Mehmet Çerçi, Zeynep Dağı, Mehmet Sait Dilek, Nevin Gaye Erbatur, Algan Hacaloğlu, Atilla Kart, Murat Mercan (chair, External Relations Committee), Mustafa Öztürk, Hüseyin Pazarcı, Ahmet Kenan Tanrıkulu, Ufuk Uras and Yaşar Yakış (chair, EU Harmonization Committee).

[2] One hundred and seventeen state officials from various state institutions in Turkey, including Ministries, Undersecretariats affiliated with the Prime Ministry, as well as the Secretariat General for EU affairs, Turkish Grand National Assembly, Turkish International Co-operation and Development Agency (TIKA), Turkish Broadcasting Agency (TRT) and Turkish Employment Organization (İŞ-KUR). Forty-six NGO members including academics, sixty-three lawyers from EU/International Relations section of Bar associations, twenty-seven foreign trade experts from several Chambers of Commerce in Turkey, five respondents from the Delegation of the EU to Turkey, one member of the Turkey–EU Joint Parliamentary Committee, one European Commission official as well as the leader of the Turkish Liberal Democratic Party.

References

Al-Wahab, I. (1979) *The Swedish Institution of Ombudsman: An Instrument of Human Rights* (Stockholm: Liberforlag).

Avşar, B. Z. (1999) *Ombudsman (Kamu Hakemi): Türkiye İçin Bir Model Önerisi [Ombudsman: A Model for Turkey]* (Ankara: Hak-İş Konfederasyonu publications).

Börzel, T. A. & Risse, T. (2000) When Europe hits home: Europeanization and domestic change, *European Integration Online Papers*, 4(15), Available at: http://eiop.or.at/eiop/texte/2000-015a.htm (accessed 6 January 2012).

Boli, John, Gallo-Cruz, Selina and Mathias. Matthew D.. (2010) "World Society, World-Polity Theory, and International Relations", in Robert Denemark (ed.), *The International Studies Encyclopedia*, Malden, MA: Blackwell Publishing.

Boyle, E. (2002) *Female Genital Cutting: Cultural Conflict in the Global Community* (Baltimore, MD & London: Johns Hopkins University Press).

Boyle, E. H. & Meyer, J. (1998) Modern law as a secularized and global model: implications for the sociology of law, *Soziale Welt*, 49(3), pp. 213–232.

Bradley, K. & Ramirez, F. O. (1996) World polity and gender parity: women's share of higher education 1965–1985, *Research in Sociology of Education and Socialization*, 11, pp. 63–91.

Buhari-Gulmez, D. (2010) Stanford School on sociological institutionalism: a global cultural approach, *International Political Sociology*, 4(3), pp. 253–270.

Cortell, A. P. & Davis, J. W. (2000) Understanding the domestic impact of international norms: a research agenda, *International Studies Review*, 2(1), pp. 65–87.

Drori, G. S. & Krücken, G. (2009) World society: a theory and research program in context, in: G. Krucken & G. S. Drori (Eds) *World Society: The Writings of John W. Meyer*, pp. 1–32 (Oxford: Oxford University Press).

Featherstone, K. & Kazamias, G. (2001) Introduction: southern Europe and the process of Europeanization, in: K. Featherstone & G. Kazamias (Eds) *Europeanization and the Southern Periphery*, pp. 1–24 (London: Frank Cass).

Featherstone, K. & Papadimitriou, D. (2008) *The Limits of Europeanization: Reform Capacity and Policy Conflict in Greece* (Basingstoke: Palgrave Macmillan).

Finnemore, M. & Sikkink, K. (1998) International norm dynamics and political change, *International Organization*, 52(4), pp. 887–917.

Gregory, R. & Giddings, P. (2002) *The Ombudsman, the Citizen and Parliament a History of the Office of the Parliamentary Commissioner for Administration and Health Service Commissioners* (London: Politico).

Hekimoğlu, I. (2000) 'Oriental Ombudsman: Advocate of public administration, but not of the people', Hurriyet Daily News, 20 September, available online at: http://www.hurriyetdailynews.com/oriental-ombudsman-advocate-of-public-administration-but-not-of-the-people.aspx?pageID=438&n=oriental-ombudsman-advocate-of-public-administration-but-not-of-the-people-2000-09-20 (accessed 31 January 2012).

Howell, K. E. (2004) Developing conceptualisations of Europeanization: synthesising methodological approaches, *Queens University On-Line Journal*, paper no. 3/2004, pp. 1–15. Available at: Available at http://www.qub.ac.uk/schools/SchoolofPoliticsInternationalStudiesandPhilosophy/FileStore/EuropeanisationFiles/Filetoupload,38403,en.pdf (accessed 31 January 2012).

Knill, C. & Lehmkuhl, D. (1999) How Europe matters: different mechanisms of Europeanization, *European Integration online Papers (EIoP)*. 3(7), Available at: http://eiop.or.at/eiop/texte/1999-007a.htm (accessed 6 January 2012)

Lechner, F. & Boli, J. (2005) *World Culture: Origins and Consequences* (Oxford: Blackwell).

Levitt, P. (2010) Not just made in the U.S.A: seeing national culture transnationally, *New Global Studies*, 4(1), Article 8. Available at: http://www.bepress.com/ngs/vol4/iss1/art8

Meyer, J. W. (1981) Kings or people, *American Journal of Sociology*, 86(4), pp. 895–899.

Meyer, J. W. (2009) Reflections: Institutional theory and world society. in: G. Krucken, G. S. Drori (Eds) *World Society: The writings of John W. Meyer*, pp. 36–63 (Oxford: Oxford University Press).

Meyer, J. W. (2001) The European Union and the globalization of culture, in: S. S. Andersen (Ed.) *Institutional Approaches to the European Union*, pp. 227–245 (Oslo: Arena).

Meyer, J. W. & Jepperson, R. (2000) The 'actors' of modern society: the cultural construction of social agency, *Sociological Theory*, 18(1), pp. 100–120.

Meyer, J. W., Boli, J., Thomas, G. & Ramirez, F. (1997) World society and the nation-state, *American Journal of Sociology*, 103(1), pp. 144–181.

Milliyet. (2011) Ombudsmanship comes from the Ottomans, 28 January, available online at: http://www.milliyet.com.tr/-ombudsmanlik-osmanli-dan-cikti-/dunya/sondakika/28.01.2011/1345419/default.htm (last accessed 31 January 2012).

Mollah, A. H. & Uddin, N. (2004) Ombudsman for Bangladesh: theory and reality, *International Journal of Public Administration*, 27(11 & 12), pp. 979–1002.

Olsen, J. (2002) The many faces of Europeanization, *Journal of Common Market Studies*, 40(5), pp. 921–952.

Özbudun, E. (2009, April 28) Kamu denetçiliği ve Anayasa Mahkemesi [State supervision and constitutional court], *Zaman newspaper*. Available at: http://www.zaman.com.tr/haber.do?haberno=842299 (accessed 31 January 2012).

Pehe, J. (1996) Elections result in surprise stalemate, *Transition*, 2(13), pp. 36–37.

Phillips, D. (2009, September 17) US analyst Phillips: Kurdish opening is a Turkish democracy initiative, *Todays Zaman*. Available at: http://www.todayszaman.com/news-187335-8-us-analyst-phillips-kurdish-opening-is-a-turkish-democracy-initiative.html (accessed 31 January 2012).

Ramirez, Francisco O. (1987) Institutional analysis. In: G. M. Thomas, J. W. Meyer, F. O. Ramirez and J. Boli (Eds) *Institutional structure*, Part 6. (Beverley Hills, CA: Sage).

Robertson, R. (1990) Mapping the global condition: globalization as the central concept, in: M. Featherstone (Ed.) *Global Culture: Nationalism Globalization and Modernity*, pp. 15–31 (London: SAGE).

Schimmelfennig, F. & Sedelmeier, U. (2005) *The Europeanization of Central and Eastern Europe* (Ithaca, NY: Cornell University Press).

Schofer, E. (2003) The global institutionalization of geological science 1800–1990, *American Sociological Review*, 68(5), pp. 730–759.

Sezen, S. (2001) Ombudsman: Türkiye İçin Nasıl Bir Çözüm? Kamu Denetçiliği Kurumu Kanunu Tasarısı Üzerine Bir Değerlendirme [Ombudsmanship: what kind of solution for Turkey? An evaluation of the draft law on public supervisory institution], *Amme İdaresi Dergisi*, 34(4), pp. 71–96.

Soysal, Y. (1994) *Limits of Citizenship: Migrants and Postnational Membership in Europe* (Chicago, IL: University of Chicago Press).

Stavridis, S. (2003) Assessing the views of academics in Greece on the Europeanisation of Greek foreign policy: a critical appraisal and a research agenda proposal, *LSE Hellenic Observatory Discussion Paper* No. 11, London, pp. 1–56. Available at: http://eprints.lse.ac.uk/5691/ (accessed 31 January 2012).

Strang, D. & Meyer, J. W. (1993) Institutional conditions for diffusion, *Theory and Society*, 22(4), pp. 487–511.

Şafaklı, O. V. (2009) Kamu Denetiminde Etkinlik Aracı Olarak 'Ombudsman' Ve AB Sürecinde KKTC'deki Uygulamaya Karşılaştırmalı Bir Bakış [Ombudsman as mechanism for state supervision and a comparative look at its implementation in the Turkish Republic of Northern Cyprus under the EU process], *Afyon Kocatepe University Journal*, XI(II), pp. 161–197.

Resisting Anamnesis: A Nietzschean Analysis of Turkey's National History Education

EDWARD WEBB*
Dickinson College, USA

ABSTRACT   The Turkish Republic that emerged from the collapsing Ottoman Empire offers an instructive example of a self-conscious deployment of history by political elites to build a nation fitting the new state. The purpose of official history has been to tie the population to the land and the State, and to the project of 'modernization' (meaning, mostly, Europeanization). It encompasses many apparent contradictions that nevertheless have had to be reconciled in the historical narratives presented to schoolchildren and what has been omitted from those narratives, such as the role of Europeans as wartime enemies versus the new Republic's European orientation. In order to explain how Turkish republican official history selectively synthesized and mobilized disparate potential historical sources of a modernizing national identity, I analyze history textbooks and curricular materials from the 1930s through the 1950s, applying a four-way analysis drawn from Nietzsche. Following the schema presented in his early essay 'History in the service and disservice of life' I show examples of how different elements of Turkey's past, as well as key events in European history, are deployed in monumental, antiquarian, and critical modes of representation. I discuss Nietzsche's main preoccupation in that essay, the importance of forgetting, and apply it to some of the occlusions in the history curriculum of the early Republic. The article sheds light on the content of the history curriculum and the challenges facing reformers today, and also illustrates an analytic schema that could be applied to other cases of national identity construction.

In an early essay, 'History in the service and disservice of life', Nietzsche (1990 [1873]) argues that history should serve the present life of an individual or nation. He rejects the notion of a 'scientific history', history for its own sake. The majority of his essay is dedicated to illuminating the dangers of history, the necessity of forgetting, and the necessity of prioritizing present life over the dead hand of the past. But he also argues that in its place history has essential purposes. Memory and forgetting are equally essential. The way the Turkish Republic has educated its citizens since the 1930s can usefully be understood as a Nietzschean project, history serving a particular vision of the national present and future. This presents both opportunities and obstacles for reform, particularly as Turkey pursues closer integration into European political structures.

Nietzsche on the Uses of History and Forgetting

In Nietzsche's view, there are three main purposes to history, and to each corresponds a particular mode:

> In three respects history is relevant to the living. It is relevant to the man of action and ambition, to the man who preserves and venerates, and to the man who suffers and needs liberation. These three relations correspond to the three kinds of history, insofar as we can distinguish between *exemplary* or *monumental*, *antiquarian*, and *critical* history. (Nietzsche, 1990, pp. 94–95)

We can readily envisage ways in which these needs can scale up to the level of a political society, in different combinations depending upon circumstance. A newly established state will surely need critical history to solidify the rupture with the past. But the new society will also need historical anchors to tie citizens to land, borders, the State, and each other, the function of antiquarian history. And building a new polity will demand forward-looking collective will, guided by exemplary role models and events.

Nietzsche also argues that forgetting is as functional and essential as remembering, possibly more so:

> it is possible to live almost without memory, indeed to live happily, as the animals show us; but without forgetting, it is utterly impossible to *live* at all. Or to make my point still clearer: *There is a degree of insomnia, of historical awareness, which injures and finally destroys a living thing, whether a man, a people, or a culture.* (Nietzsche, 1990, pp. 89–90, emphases in original)

Total recall is disabling, immobilizing. Anamnesis, failing to forget, can be dangerous for the health of humans and societies alike. In this pragmatic approach to history, what is not useful to present and future life is to be abandoned to the past.

Operationalizing Nietzsche's Four Categories

> Every man, every nation, requires, according to its goals, strengths, and necessities, a certain knowledge of the past, a knowledge now in the form of exemplary history, now of antiquarian history, and now of critical history. (Nietzsche, 1990, p. 103)

Where history is put in the service of nationalism we might reasonably expect to find all three of Nietzsche's approved uses of history as well as forgetting, in combinations that differ according to particular circumstance. Contrary to the aspiration of 'scientific' history rejected by Nietzsche for a knowledge broadly value-free, projects of national identity formation and reproduction demand that history serve as a mirror of desired national *values*—it is values that will determine what knowledge is deemed useful to the formation of citizens. Given that priority, the content associated with each mode seems likely to be as follows:

- *Monumental* history provides landmarks, inspirational figures and events for citizens to emulate. Expected content would be accounts of leaders, martyrs, battles, major contributions to science and culture, possibly monuments in the literal sense.

- *Antiquarian* history can supply heritage, whereby citizens learn their place in world history. This could be particularly important in new states or polities, naturalizing citizens' ties to the territory of a new state, 'right-sizing' the imaginary of the people.[1] Expected content would be earlier worthy civilizations that can be connected to the present society either by geography or ancestry.

These first two modes are about elements of history kept alive in the present for the purposes of the future. They show what of the past is worthy to be brought into the present, through emulation and celebration. They *affirm* elements of the past. The remaining modes *negate*, treating those things of the past that are to be repudiated or forgotten, staying in the past:

> it is clear how urgently man often needs to supplement the exemplary and antiquarian modes of viewing the past with a *third*, the *critical* mode; and that he needs this too in life's service. In order to live, man must possess the strength, and occasionally employ it, to shatter and disintegrate a past. (Nietzsche, 1990, p. 102)

The critical mode is clearly about action. Amnesia is less obviously so in an individual. But at a social level, amnesia can involve active choices about what is left out of history texts and even active suppression of memory:

- *Critical* history performs a crucial boundary-setting role, showing what of the past must be left in the past; here the expected content would be accounts of the failings of previous polities and possibly useful 'others' in the form of enemy states or peoples.
- *Amnesia* insulates the body politic against remorse and self-doubt, against 'insomnia' in Nietzsche's term. In the case of nationalist histories, among the things to be forgotten will be events and identities that trouble the dominant narrative of peoplehood and national unity. Amnesiac history is hardest to find, of course, since its marker is the *absence* of content. The main analytic resource would be histories written from the perspective of history as an end in itself. What do such histories contain of significance that is absent in the official narrative?

A likely distinction between the targeted 'other' of critical and amnesiac modes is the distinction between external and internal others. Critical history can usefully target the *ancien regime* which, by definition, is no longer part of the nation and polity, and external enemies which either never were part or have ceased to be—historic rivals and secessionist groups help to define who 'we' are not. 'Others' who remain within are a harder challenge for unitary nationalism, so the easier mode of negation is erasure.

Table 1 summarizes the orientation of each mode according to two criteria: whether they affirm or negate the past, claiming some for the self, rejecting some as other; and whether their main use is in promoting change or the status quo.

A well-established society and polity presumably has less need of such ideological tools. En route to a society confident enough for a more 'scientific history' such as Nietzsche

Table 1. The relationship of modes of history to the past

	Change	Status quo
Affirmation/self	Monumental	Antiquarian
Negation/other	Critical	Amnesiac

rejects, antiquarian history might become more prominent as the need for the outsized heroes of monumental history and cartoon villains of critical history recedes. Those two modes are useful for action and change; antiquarian history is the history of the status quo, quietist history suited to an established society. Nietzsche (1990, p. 100) argues 'that antiquarian sense of historical reverence is of the greatest value when it fills the modest, coarse, even miserable conditions in which a man or a nation lives, with a simple, poignant feeling of pleasure and contentment'. The amnesiac mode also, logically, supports the status quo.

In the longer run, a greater degree of self-confidence might imply not only less need to resort to the critical othering of previous regimes or rival peoples, but also the possibility of *self*-criticism, something that may in turn involve anamnesis, the recovery of suppressed memories. We can imagine a general model of nationalist history projects that looks something like this:

- Foundation period: Monumental, Antiquarian, Critical, Amnesiac all widely deployed.
- Consolidation period: Monumental and Critical lessen in importance; Antiquarian and Amnesiac dominant.
- Maturity: 'Scientific' history can successfully compete with nationalist history; possibility of Anamnesis.

But there is no reason to suppose this process to be either inevitable or unidirectional. The citizenship tests that have been introduced into various European and other societies in the past few years could be read as including the return of elements of nationalist history, specifically the revival of value-laden monumental and antiquarian narratives, as multi-cultural models of immigration give way to an emerging policy consensus on the desirability of acculturation (Wright, 2008). On the other hand, in the case of Turkey official history education has remained essentially static over the life of the Republic, with little erosion of its monumental and critical elements, and a determined effort on the part of the State to enforce amnesia about politically sensitive topics. Only recently do we see attempts to begin reform of the curriculum and efforts such as those undertaken by the European Association of History Educators, EUROCLIO, to promote alternatives to nationalist history education, broaching topics that 'cannot be learned' such as Turkey's history since the death of Ataturk in 1938 or the diverse origins of modern Turks (Saydam, 2009; Smart, 2009).[2]

How the Turkish Republic Has Used History

The four modes of history could be used to enable systematic cross-case comparison. Here Turkey serves as an illustration of how they can be applied analytically.

The founder of the Turkish Republic, Mustafa Kemal Pasha, later Ataturk, was probably more influenced by French than German thought: his approach to the relationship of religion to the State strongly resembled French *laîcité*, for example. But his approach to history was robustly Nietzschean. One of his aphorisms adorns the entrance to the reading room at the Republican Archives in Ankara: 'Writing history is as important as making it.' The practices of the Republic under his rule make clear that the history envisaged is very much in the service of (the nation's) life. History was subordinated to the emergent ideology of Kemalism as the founding generation pursued an ambitious program of both statebuilding and nationbuilding:

if historical scholarship is to be a beneficent enterprise, holding future promise, it must itself move in the wake of a fresh and powerful torrent of life—for instance, a newly emerging culture. History, therefore, must be guided and controlled by a higher power and must not itself guide and control. (Nietzsche, 1990, p. 94)[3]

In 1931 and 1932 Kemal created cultural foundations to construct an ideological framework for the Republic, and maintained an active role in both for the remainder of his life: the *Türk Tarih Kurumu* and *Türk Dil Kurumu*, the Turkish History and Language Foundations (Taşkın, 2001). Influenced by their work, government institutions of the Republic supported an official history that projected backwards a distinctive and coherent narrative of Turkish peoplehood and looked forwards confidently to a leading place in modernity, as part of world civilization understood in terms of post-Enlightenment Europe. To a great extent, that narrative and historic framing have persisted into the contemporary history and social studies curricula, with the addition only of some Islamic history in the 1970s (Aktekin, 2009, p. 26). History as it is taught in Turkey has remained largely history as 'guided and controlled' by the higher power of Kemalist orthodoxy.

To understand the content of the history deployed in the service of Kemalist goals I examined textbooks and curricular materials in what might be termed the foundational and consolidation periods of the Republic: the 1930s, when Kemal's foundations began their work and educational reforms introduced in the 1920s began to have nation-wide impact; and the 1950s, when the first multi-party democracy experiment took place and the more socially conservative Democrat Party was in power.[4] Nietzsche's modes all appear active in the ideological project.

The Antiquarian and the Monumental

There is little doubt that the production of a national history, distinct from 'scientific' history, was a self-conscious process on the part of education officials and textbook authors. We can see a mixture of *antiquarian* and *monumental* or exemplary thinking in a mid-1930s history text:

> As for the aim of national history, it is to make the new generation love their homeland, to acquaint them with the most respected nations and inculcate in them the heroism and virtues of their ancestors. The goal of national education is not to know the past, it is the art of making the future. (Behnan, 1934, p. 355)

The author understands the purpose of all education in the Republic to be 'to produce young citizens who will be useful to the Turkish homeland, the Turkish nation, Turkish society' (Behnan, 1934, p. 358). This is straightforwardly Nietzschean. Behnan and other authors worked consistently within this ideological framework throughout the first few decades of the Republic. The foreword to Ahmet Refik's (1932, p. 3) book for fourth years, for example, explains that in the book,

> Turkey's history is rescued from being the history of the sultans. Rather, it is written with attention to all the Turkish nation. Among historical events, especially those pertaining to the evolution of the Turks are chosen. In order to be exemplars to children, importance is given to showing how the most steadfast great men among the Turks in art, science, heroism, and administering Turkey have caused Turkish civilization to progress.

In the 1934 book, Behnan notes that under the Empire history had been taught as if it started with the first Ottomans in the thirteenth century. Whereas Turkish history is both deeper and broader—after all, 'the Turks are among the most ancient known civilized people on the face of the Earth' (Behnan, 1934, p. 356). He praises Kemal for his leadership of the Foundation for the Study of Turkish History which has 'begun to work to bring our national history into the full light of day' (Behnan, 1934, p. 357). This is an early appearance of the Turkish History Thesis that claims that long before the Ottoman Empire Turks had founded a civilization in Central Asia that was the source of many other civilizations: 'The aim of this thesis was to show that Anatolia has been a Turkish homeland since antiquity and all early Anatolian civilizations of Hittites, Phyrigians, Lydians, Greeks etc, were Turkish civilizations' (Aktekin, 2010, p. 26).

Thus Behnan's textbook establishes a narrative of ancient, wise, well-ordered Turkish societies corrupted over time by alien, particularly Arab, accretions. The Republic can thus appear as both modern and a return to Turkish roots. In discussing reforms concerning the role of religion in society, for instance, the author claims the following:

> In the states they founded, the ancient Turks did not get mixed up in religious affairs. They left the people free in their own faiths. The kings of some Turkish states named themselves God's deputy, for this reason they foundered, and for this reason the Ottoman Empire collapsed. (Behnan, 1934, pp. 344–345)

In a 1953 middle school textbook, the line is held: 'The great Turkish states from the earliest ages showed respect to everyone's religious beliefs' and continued to do so after accepting Islam (Inal, 1953, p. 214).

Likewise on gender: 'Among the ancient Turks there was no separation of woman and man' and this continued into the early period after the Turks adopted Islam. It was the Ottomans who separated the sexes with the introduction of the harem. The Republic has made things right with the Civil Code and the opportunities available to women (Behnan, 1934, pp. 347–348).

Refik's book similarly takes the antiquarian approach to construct a lineage for the Turks from Central Asia to Anatolia, combined with monumental history, giants such as Attila the Hun co-opted to add an heroic lustre to that heritage.

The ancient Turkish civilization narrative is antiquarian, claiming revered ancestors for present society and institutions. But there is a tension between claims of the virtues of ancient Turks as the origins of republican progress, and the obvious European provenance of much of the aesthetic, scientific and political direction of the Republic. Partly this could be reconciled by the Turkish history thesis: 'since all Antique civilizations of the world had been created by Turks, the modern western civilizations also owed much to the Turks and there is no reason to exclude the Turks from the west' (Aktekin, 2010, p. 26). But Kemal and his collaborators wished to claim Enlightenment figures and positivism as part of the Turkish story. For that there had to be recourse to further monumental thinking, presenting the forward-looking leadership of the Republic as exemplary leaders inspired in turn by the best exemplars of European progress.

In the foreword of Refik's (1932, p. 3) book, he says: 'In the history of European states, we have endeavored to explain to children in particular how today's Europe came into being, and how constitutional, republican, and nationalist sentiments began'. We can see how events and individuals from Europe's past can then play a monumental role, showing the way to a desirable future for Turkey. The curriculum was limited in which elements of Europe's history were to be taught. For example, the 1949 middle school curriculum includes only the following, limited European components after Year 1 (when ancient Mediterranean civilizations appear alongside Central Asia). Year 2 begins with 'A general look at the Middle Ages in the West' making up 5–6 per cent of the material to be covered that year. In Year 3 there is more, but tellingly selective. The year opens with a section (one of eleven) on early modern Europe, covering scientific and technological advancements, major geographical discoveries, the Renaissance, and the Reformation. Section Six is on seventeenth- and eighteenth-century Europe and (North) America, covering in three subsections the principal European states, the foundation of the USA, and the causes and effects of the French Revolution. Europe is of course involved in later events covered by the syllabus, including the World Wars and Turkey's War of Liberation, but does not appear as a separate topic or subtopic in the syllabus (TC Milli Eğitim Bakanlığı, 1949, pp. 95–100). Textbook coverage of the events selected here—Renaissance, Reformation, Revolution—is in approving terms, with figures such as Luther and Robespierre singled out for attention (and in some books, illustration). It is affirming, monumental.

Criticism and Amnesia—the Others of Kemalist Nationalism

In covering the foundation of the Republic, textbooks tend to pair the monumental and the critical. Here the earlier approval of certain European figures and events drops away. Europeans collectively appear in the guise of villains. Refik's chapters on the period between the restoration of the Ottoman Constitution in 1908 and the creation of the Republic lay out the nationalist narrative clearly (1932, pp. 129–142). Taking advantage of a weak government, 'the Turks' enemies said "this is a great opportunity"'. The Balkans rise, the Italians take the last Turkish possessions in North Africa, the Serbs, Bulgarians and Greeks unite to attack the Turks, taking all the Balkans: 'they left only Edirne in our hands' (Refik, 1932, p. 129). The identity evoked is 'Turks', not Ottomans.

The account of the First World War portrays Mustafa Kemal Pasha as a bold leader of the 'heroic Turks' who fight like lions. The Union & Progress government makes peace with the British, who promise not to occupy Istanbul but break their word. The capital fills with enemy soldiers, much to the delight of 'the Christians living in Turkey' (excluded by that terminology from membership in the nation) who fraternize with the British and French occupiers (Refik, 1932, p. 131). The Arabs bloodily eject the Turks from their lands: 'The Christians living in the Ottoman Empire were together with the enemy. The British robbed the man in the street. They shared out all of Turkey. They inserted the Greeks into Izmir, and killed our officers and soldiers' (Refik, 1932, p. 132).

This is a deeply unflattering portrait of the European powers, and it clearly implicates non-Muslim Anatolians in the Empire's ultimate collapse. All the named enemies are Europeans and/or Christians, with a small role for the Arabs. It is relentless, almost claustrophobic, providing a darkness from which Kemal can rescue the nation.

This is the Treaty of Sèvres moment, the start of the process whereby, in nationalist history, Kemal leads the besieged and friendless Turks from deceit and betrayal by European enemies without and non-Turkish enemies within through violent struggle to birth as a nation and a modern state. In the following chapter the 'bold hero' Mustafa Kemal Pasha delivers the nation from the foreign enemy. The last couple of pages describe the declaration of the Republic and the spread of schools, railroads, public gardens and freedom throughout Anatolia. The style throughout these last two short chapters is clearly monumental. The Turks undergo existential struggle led by towering heroes against faceless enemies, who appear only in the anonymous plural—the Greeks, the British, the Christians, the Armenians, the Arabs.

The War of Independence left Turks particularly sensitive on the issue of territorial integrity and sovereignty, with the State vigilant to the point of paranoia about potential threats from within and without. National unity became a core value. Rather than solutions that might 'right-size the State' to take account of the religious, ethnic, and linguistic diversity of the new Republic, it was the people that must be 'right-sized' to conform to the territory through education and cultural politics. Citizens of the new Republic were to be understood as homogeneous Turks—speaking a common language, following (as private citizens) Sunni Islam, and attached to the territory of Anatolia (or Eastern Thrace, the only part of continental Europe remaining under Turkish control). The dissonance between mythical homogeneity and actual diversity led to repressive measures as Turkishness was defined and imposed.

Official Turkishness had geographic, racial and religious characteristics. The geographic element caused difficulties for Kemal himself, since he was born in the Balkans. In late 1922, he faced a challenge to his continuing role in Grand National Assembly. A draft amendment to the electoral law would disqualify from candidacy those born outside Turkey's borders at the time, unless they had been resident for five years in a constituency. Kemal was the obvious target, but the purpose of the amendment as explained by the leader of the opposition in the Assembly was that it was meant to exclude Arabs or Albanians, but allow 'Turkish or Kurdish' refugees to achieve eligibility through residence (Mango, 2002, p. 369). The majority of members of all four groups were Sunni Muslims. The differences are geographical—to the extent that Anatolia is home to Turks and Kurds, members of those groups from elsewhere could make some claim to belonging, while Arabs and Albanians were to be understood as other. The Kurds were later to disappear from official consideration, absorbed into Turkish identity in official discourse.

There was also a racial consciousness at work in the construction of Turkish nationalism in the 1920s and 1930s. Despite their pride in their Central Asian origins, Turks' aspirations to membership in European civilization led to an attribution of 'whiteness'. In April 1932 a memo from the Presidency to the Prime Minister's office ordered an end to the use of an atlas published the previous year that had numerous 'errors' in it, including the attribution of Turks to the 'yellow race' whereas 'the editors will be able to see that this is incorrect simply by looking around themselves.' The errors in the atlas are attributed in the memo to it having been translated from a foreign source which clearly was 'a long way from new scientific bases'.[5] That the Presidency had time to concern itself with such matters is a sign of the priority Kemal put on education for Turkish identity-production.

The Ottoman Empire appears in the curriculum in monumental mode in its early years and at its peak, and in critical mode in the centuries of decline. It is depicted as a great Turkish civilizational achievement, undone by scheming rival powers as it was weakened by the 'backwardness' of the religious mentality: European states and traditional Islamic practices are both the targets of critical history. Some texts make a clear identification of modern Turks with the Empire:

> In the Reform Period quite a few internal rebellions broke out in *our* country. Nations who were not Turkish began movements to separate from *our* rule. Carried away by the ideas of nationalism and freedom spread by the French Revolution, they

wanted to found independent states. The Russians and other Europeans encouraged them ... The Greeks, like the Serbs, revolted in order to separate from *us*. (Oktay, 1956, pp. 98–99, emphases added)

Even in 1950s textbooks, under a Democrat Party that was more sympathetic to religious conservatism, the role of religion in education, law, and government is presented as alien and damaging. The hat law (abolishing the fez) and closure of the religious orders are presented as driven by the incompatibility of these things with modernity. Changes to the calendar, numbers, weights and measures are presented as adopting 'western' and 'international' standards and leaving behind 'Muslim' and 'old' standards. Turkishness and modernity are separated from Muslimness.

Back in the 1930s, Behnan was hostile and dismissive toward the system of religious law under the Empire, attributing it to Arab influence:

In the old courts the judges passed judgment according to *şeriat*. By *şeriat* is meant a bunch of rules made according to the customs of desert Arabs twelve centuries before. The *nizamiye* courts [those created by nineteenth-century reforms] also took a bunch of rules from religion. These Arab rules could not secure the customs of a modern Turkish society. (Behnan, 1934, p. 345)

Furthermore, Christians' legal affairs were overseen by priests, and foreigners ran their own courts, hence the 1926 civil code and the end of separate courts for Christians. A 1953 middle school textbook, produced under the Democrat Party government, has a similar narrative with a minor twist: 'the minorities *wanted* to give up their own justice and have their affairs overseen by Turkish courts' (Inal, 1953, p. 215, emphasis added). A simpler text for the final year of primary school in 1954 does not mention the minorities issue explicitly when discussing the legal revolution, merely noting the closure of *şeriat* courts and saying all citizens could now be judged in the same place and according to the same laws (Yener, 1954, p. 189).

The Arabs were not the only group among the former Ottoman subjects to see their historic achievements dismissed or erased, of course. Salah ad-Din, the liberator of Jerusalem from the Crusaders is a significant hero in Middle Eastern culture. He was of Kurdish origin, except in Turkish nationalist historiography, where he is a Turk. A textbook published in 1957 says Salah ad-Din was 'the son of Eyyub, a Turkish commander' and that only the Turks stood against the Crusaders to defend the lands of Islam: 'Were it not for the Turks, the Crusaders would have taken over all of Anatolia, Syria, Palestine and Egypt' (Akın & Uluçay, 1957, pp. 94, 96). Here is a double feat of Nietzschean history making: amnesia erases Salah ad-Din's Kurdish identity; monumentalism makes him a Turkish hero.

The Birth of 'Sèvres Syndrome'

The general thrust of the reforms of the 1920s and 1930s was toward unity and uniformity in all aspects of national life, and textbooks present this as unambiguously positive. There are some minor exceptions to the large picture of homogeneity:

In the time of the Ottoman state the Christian and Jewish minorities had schools. These schools taught what they wanted to. The state couldn't inspect them: after the

Treaty of Lausanne these schools were adapted to the Turkish system. Turkish teachers teach Turkish, civics and history. These are under Education Ministry control as private schools. (Behnan, 1934, p. 357)

In this brief account we have reflections of many of the anxieties of Turkish nationalists at the time—those minorities teach *what they like* and *unsupervised*. This was an affront to national sovereignty and security. After Lausanne, minorities were to be monitored and inoculated with Turkish, Civics, and History. Suspicion of the other within is mollified by the oversight of the State, and by the presence of Turks in the classroom. Sèvres gives way to Lausanne, the threat of partition is averted; national unity asserts itself.

Celebrating the Treaty of Lausanne and the establishment of the Republic involves remembering what preceded it. The Treaty of Sèvres, attempting to dismember all but the core of the Ottoman lands and share them out among external enemies and their minority clients within, is an essential monument on the terrain of Turkish national consciousness. It is the touchstone of nationalist paranoia, evoked in the 'Operation Sèvres' of the bestselling political thriller *Metal Fırtına* in which the USA seeks to occupy and divide Turkey to the benefit of Armenians and others (Uçar & Turna, 2004). Sèvres makes Europe and minorities *eternal others* of the Republic. The minorities who departed are remembered, in hostile terms: the exchange of populations with Greece is mentioned in many textbooks as an essential and positive part of Lausanne. The others have been subject for years to official forgetting: Kurds, Alevis and others.

Today Turkey's national consciousness appears to retain the marks of the contradictory monuments of the founding moment. While Turkey pursues closer integration into European structures, scholars also speak of 'Sèvres Syndrome', an abiding suspicion of western desire to divide Turkey (Yılmaz, 2006; Wigen, 2009). It may have what could be termed the 'Lausanne Corollary', a passionate insistence on the homogeneity of the citizens of the Republic, since the troublesome (non-Muslim) minorities were removed in an internationally approved operation of ethnic cleansing by forced population exchange (Clark, 2006). Such a corollary demands amnesia about the minorities who remain.

Challenges of Moving toward Anamnesis

Turkish history and social studies teachers and, especially, student teachers surveyed in late 2008 and early 2009 not only oppose Turkey's ambitions to join the EU but by very clear margins oppose the teaching of European history. As Saydam (2009: 41) puts it, 'Having a negative perspective concerning the EU on the grounds of political choice is one thing and not wanting to learn or to teach about European history in the class is another thing'. They are different, yet may be intimately connected. If the aim of history teaching is, as Turkish law still says, 'To train all members of the Turkish Nation as citizens who believe in the principles and reforms of Ataturk' and so on, then choices of what is included in the curriculum as well as how it is taught remain saturated with ideological values.[6] Turkish history education remains fundamentally Nietzschean, designed to promote nationalism through deployment of the monumental, antiquarian, critical, and amnesiac modes.

As long ago as 1949, UNESCO issued guidelines connecting 'narrowly conceived national history' to conflict (Schissler, 2005, p. 236). Reform toward more cosmopolitan education has made some inroads in Turkey as elsewhere, particularly in Council of Europe member states. But 'in spite of recent attempts, the commanding presence of bureaucratic machinery involved in curriculum development makes reform a slow and unavailing process' (Antoniou & Nuhoğlu Soysal, 2005, p. 109). Attempts such as those in the EUROCLIO project to recover memory, to promote counter-narratives that challenge cherished myths of ethnic and cultural homogeneity or a particular civilizational trajectory, will inevitably encounter substantial resistance:

> teachers and student teachers cannot help but evaluate the developments of the 2000s with the viewpoints of the 1920s. Those who prefer to place Turkey in the geography of Europe in such areas as sports, music, fashion, and cinema act differently when it comes to politics, the independence of the country, mutual inspection, and cooperation of states. (Saydam, 2009, p. 43)

Notes

[1] On the concept of 'rightsizing the state' see O'Leary et al. (2002).
[2] Saydam calls the second half of the twentieth century the topic that can't be learned. Even today the history curriculum for all but the small minority of students who study History in Year 12 stops at the Second World War. The curriculum as established under Ataturk focusing on ancient Turks, the Ottomans, Enlightenment Europe and the establishment of the Republic is what students in upper primary and secondary education study in social studies and history classes. Turkey's history as a democracy punctuated by coups, its experiences as a member of NATO, the rise of political Islam and Kurdish nationalism are all outside the curriculum. Information about EUROCLIO's Turkey project can be found at http://www.euroclio.eu/site/index.php/projects-mainmenu-125/current-projects-mainmenu-32/turkey-mainmenu-855.
[3] In this, Turkey is quite typical among modernizing nation-states of the late nineteenth and early twentieth centuries—see Schissler and Soysal (2005), especially 'Introduction: teaching beyond the national narrative', pp. 1–9.
[4] I reviewed twenty-three Turkish history textbooks in the Georg Eckert Institute collection published between 1931 and 1959. I am confident that they are representative of textbooks of the period due to the strong direction of the State in setting the curriculum and approving any text to be used in schools. All quote the relevant law and cite Ministry of Education approval in their front matter.
[5] Turkish Republic, Prime Ministry Republican Archives (Başbakanlık Cumhuriyet Arşivi) 030.10.144.31.4.
[6] Basic Law of National Education no. 1739 of 1973 as amended by Law no. 2842 of 1989. For a translation see Aktekin (2009, pp. 24–25).

References

Akın, H. & Uluçay, M. Ç. (1957) *İlkokul Kitapları—Tarih—Sınıf IV* (Istanbul: İnkılâp Kitabevi).
Aktekin, S. (2009) History education in Turkey, in: S. Aktekin, P. Harnett, M. Öztürk & D. Smart (Eds) *Teaching History and Social Studies for Multicultural Europe*, pp. 23–39 (Ankara: Harf Eğitim Yayıncılığı).
Antoniou, V. L. & Nuhoğlu Soysal, Y. (2005) Nation and the other in Greek and Turkish history textbooks, in: H. Schissler & Y. Nuhoğlu Soysal (Eds) *The Nation, Europe, and the World*, pp. 105–121 (Oxford: Berghahn Books).
Behnan, E. (1934) *Tarih Bakaloryası—Osmanlı ve Cumhuriyet Tarihi* (Ankara: Suhulet Kutuphanesi).
Clark, B. (2006) *Twice a Stranger* (Cambridge, MA: Harvard University Press).
Inal, A. E. (1953) *Tarih—Orta: III* (Istanbul: Atlas Yayınevi).
Mango, A. (2002) *Atatürk: The Biography of the Founder of Modern Turkey* (Woodstock: Overlook Press).
Nietzsche, F. (1990 [1873]) History in the service and disservice of life, in: W. Arrowsmith, (Ed.) (trans. G. Brown) *Unmodern Observations*, pp. 87–145 (New Haven, CT: Yale University Press).
Oktay, E. (1956) *Yeni Tarih Dersleri V* (Istanbul: Remzi Kitabevi).
O'Leary, B., Lustick, I. S. & Callaghy, T. (Eds) (2002) *Rightsizing the State* (Oxford: Oxford University Press).

Refik, A. (1932) *Çocuklara Tarih Bilgisi—Eskizamanlar: Türkler* (Istanbul: Hilmi Kitaphanesi).
Saydam, A. (2009) The century that cannot be learned: teaching of XXth century in Turkey, in: S. Aktekin, P. Harnett, M. Öztürk & D. Smart (Eds) *Teaching History and Social Studies for Multicultural Europe*, pp. 41–58 (Ankara: Harf Eğitim Yayıncılığı).
Schissler, H. (2005) World history: making sense of the present, in: H. Schissler & Y. Nuhoğlu Soysal (Eds) *The Nation, Europe, and the World*, pp. 228–245 (Oxford: Berghahn Books).
Schissler, H. & Nuhoğlu Soysal, Y. (Eds) (2005) *The Nation, Europe, and the World* (Oxford: Berghahn Books).
Smart, D. (2009) The origins of modern Turkey, in: S. Aktekin, P. Harnett, M. Öztürk & D. Smart (Eds) *Understanding Ourselves and One Another: Active Learning for History and Social Studies Lessons*, pp. 101–116 (Ankara: Harf Eğitim Yayıncılığı).
Taşkın, Y. (2001) Kemalist Kültür Politikaları Açısından Türk Tarih ve Dil Kurumları, in: A. Insel (Ed.) *Modern Türkiye'de Siyasî Düşünce, Cilt 2: Kemalizm*, pp. 419–424 (Istanbul: İletişim).
TC Milli Eğitim Bakanlığı (1949) *Orta Okul Programı* (Ankara: Milli Eğitim Basımevi).
Uçar, O. & Turna, B. (2004) *Metal Fırtına* (Istanbul: Timaş Yayınları).
Wigen, E. (2009) *A Turkish Mission Civilisatrice in Iraq?* Paper delivered at the Annual Convention of the International Studies Association, 15–18 February, New York City.
Wright, S. (2008) Citizenship tests in Europe—editorial introduction, *International Journal on Multicultural Societies*, 10(1), pp. 1–9.
Yener, C. (1954) *İlkokul Kitapları—Tarih—5. Sınıf* (Istanbul: Ahmet Halit Yaşaroğlu).
Yılmaz, M. H. (2006) Two pillars of Nationalist Euroskepticism in Turkey: the Tanzimat and Sèvres Syndromes, in: I. Karlsson & A. Strom Melin (Eds) *Turkey, Sweden and the European Union: Experiences and Expectations*, pp. 29–40 (Stockholm: Swedish Institute for European Policy Studies).

A Bakhtinian Approach to EU–Turkey Relations

JOHANNA NYKÄNEN*
University of Warwick, UK

ABSTRACT *This article proposes that dialogue between the EU and its candidate countries should be institutionalised in the EU accession framework. Using Mikhail Bakhtin's concept of dialogism, it argues that the current deadlock in EU–Turkey accession negotiations is partly due to a lack of genuine dialogue between the parties. In the current structure, Turkey has been finalised, closed and determined in its image as the ultimate other vis-à-vis Europe. For the relations between the EU and Turkey to move forward, Turkey should be allowed to speak and answer back in the formal framework of the accession process.*

Introduction

There is something uncanny about the candidate negotiations between the EU and Turkey. One gets a feeling that something is not quite right. In addition to the sensitive political issues—such as the Cyprus question—and identity questions that concern Turkey's European credentials, there is a prevalent feeling of uneasiness surrounding the negotiations. This feeling of uneasiness translates into accusations of the EU treating Turkey *unfairly*, and is prevalent in Turkey, the EU as well as in the USA. Ankara has repeatedly argued that there are unfair obstacles put in Turkey's way (see, for example, *Journal of Turkish Weekly*, 2006). NATO, similarly, accuses the EU of treating Turkey in an unfair manner (*Hürriyet Daily News*, 7 July 2010). In Europe, the Independent Commission on Turkey has talked about the unfair EU–Turkey accession process, arguing in its 2009 report that unfair obstacles have been put in Turkey's path to the EU.[1] This view is rampant also among political commentators (see, for example, Ellemann-Jensen, 2006). The EU's actions are often attributed to its lack of strategic thinking. As Kader Sevinc (2010, p. 96) argues, 'lack of political leadership and strategic vision has caused the continuing membership negotiations between Turkey and the EU to become a bit of an enigma, rather than an end-game'.

As Elisabeth Johansson-Nogues and Ann-Kristin Jonasson (2011, p. 113) point out, the analysis of the bumpy Turkish EU accession reform process has largely been steeped either in a Rational Institutionalist logic of 'opportunity costs' both for the EU and for Turkey, or assessed as a question of the Turkish (in)compatibility with European values. While drawing from both the approaches, this article attempts to untangle the question by approaching it from the perspective of Mikhail Bakhtin. While at first it may seem far-fetched to use Bakhtin's ideas in the context of EU–Turkey relations, this article aims to show—with the conscious risk of reproducing an intellectual cliché[2]—that they can offer new insights to the topic. To apply Bakhtin's work in the discipline of International Relations (IR) is not a novel enterprise. Iver Neumann (1999), for example, discusses Bakhtin in his seminal work on otherness in IR. Prior to Neumann, Richard K. Ashley (in Der Derian & Shapiro (eds) 1989) dealt with Bakhtin's concepts of dialogue-monologue nexus, and Michael J. Shapiro (ibid) with heteroglossia within the IR field. Later treatment of Bakhtin in IR include Xavier Guillaume (2002) who attempted to develop a dialogical understanding of International Relations within the meta-theoretical field of constructivism.

Explaining Bakhtin

The starting point of Bakhtin's theory of dialogism is familiar to every student of the Constructivist branch of International Relations theory. In short, Bakhtin argues that the 'other' is pivotal in the construction of the 'self'. Without the other, the subject cannot know either itself or the world because meaning is created in discourse where consciousnesses meet (Neumann, 1999, p. 13). Selfhood is something that is given by one consciousness to another. As Bakhtin (1990, pp. 35–36) writes:

> One can speak of a human being's absolute need for the other, for the other's seeing, remembering, gathering, and unifying self-activity—the only self-activity capable of producing his outwardly finished personality. This outward personality could not exist, if the other did not create it.

In this article, the EU is analysed as the 'self' and Turkey as the 'other' through Bakhtin's thesis on Dostoevsky's 'author' and 'hero'. This is not to deny agency to Turkey but to narrow the topic down to a Bakhtinian approach in which an author creates his/her characters and heroes. Indeed, while it is perhaps worth noting that, as Alastair Bonnett (2004) argues, also Turkey needed to invent the West in order to invent itself, in the context of EU–Turkey accession negotiations the EU has technically *created* Turkey as a *candidate country*. Without the EU Turkey would not exist as a candidate state for EU membership. Bakhtin (1984, p. 65) writes that:

> it might seem that the independence of a character contradicts the fact that he exists, entirely and solely, as an aspect of a work of art, and consequently is wholly created from beginning to end by the author. In fact there is no such contradiction ... each (hero) has its own order, his own logic, which enters into the realm of the author's whim. Once he has chosen a hero and the dominant of his hero's representation, the author is already bound by the inner logic of what he has chosen, and he must reveal it in his representation.

Indeed, as Bakhtin (1984, p. 65) continues,

> to create does not mean to invent. Every creative act is bound by its own special laws, as well as by the laws of the material with which it works. Every creative act is

determined by its object and by the structure of its object, and therefore permits no arbitrariness; in essence it invents nothing, but only reveals what is already present in the object itself.

The EU created the institutional animal of Turkey as a candidate state, but there still exists—outside this object—an independent and sovereign entity called Turkey. The EU's authorial position only reaches as far as that bureaucratic exercise called an accession process.

According to Bakhtin, interaction between the 'self' and the 'other' takes place through discourse, which is made up of utterances. *Utterance* is a key concept in Bakhtin's dialogism. As Bakhtin (1986, p. 92) explains:

> The expression of an utterance always responds to a greater or lesser degree, that is, it expresses the speaker's attitude toward others' utterances and not just his attitude toward the object of his utterance ... However monological the utterance may be ..., however much it may concentrate on its own object, it cannot but be, in some measure, a response to what has already been said about the given topic, on the given issue, even though this responsiveness may not have assumed a clear-cut external expression ... The utterance is filled with dialogic overtones, and they must be taken into account in order to understand fully the style of the utterance.

Bakhtin distinguishes between two levels within an utterance. The first level, as Guillaume (2002, p. 6) writes,

> is constituted by *dialogism per se*, that is, the universal process through which we can actually give meaning to utterances by their interweaving. The second level is *the characterisation of the utterance*, that is to say, in a Bakhtinian perspective, in the style it possesses, which in turn reflects figurations of otherness. In other words, it is a matter of evaluating the extent to which the other is taken into account in an utterance.

In short, a Bakhtinian view of utterance includes both the language itself and the way it is interpreted in action, as an answerable act. In dialogism there is always room for debate. This article focuses on the latter level, analysing the style of the EU's utterances towards Turkey.

As stated earlier, the addressivity of an utterance is its essential quality. This addressee, Bakhtin (1986, pp. 93–95) writes,

> can be an immediate participant-interlocutor in an everyday dialogue, ... a more or less differentiated public, ethnic group, contemporaries, like-minded people, opponents and enemies ... And it can also be an indefinite, unconcretized other ... both the composition and, particularly, the style of the utterance depend on those to whom the utterance is addressed, how the speaker (or writer) senses and imagines his addressees, and the force of their effect on the utterance.

As such, dialogism is not restricted to individuals but can concern, as in the case of this article, actors in IR, for example.

The inbuilt responsiveness in every utterance has particular importance in relation to EU–Turkey relations. This will be further elaborated later on in the article. What is important here now is to note that a dialogic relationship is an ideal form of interaction between two sides with a *monologist* discourse being its very antithesis. Monologism

> at its extreme, denies the existence outside itself of another consciousness with equal rights and equal responsibilities, another *I* with equal rights ... With a monologic approach (in its extreme or pure form) *another person* remains wholly and merely an *object* of consciousness, and not another consciousness ... Monologue is finalised and deaf to the other's response, does not expect it and does not acknowledge it in any *decisive* force. Monologue manages without the other, and therefore to some degree materialises all reality. Monologue pretends to be the *ultimate word*. It closes down the represented world and represented persons. (Bakhtin, 1984, pp. 292–293)

EU–Turkey Relations—Negotiations without Dialogue

One might wonder whether arguing that EU–Turkey relations are lacking in dialogue is not an obvious statement. After all, with their history of enmity and current asymmetric power relations, it would be only natural that the politically and economically mightier party dictated the process. Yet, this is far from palpable. Putting aside the fact that the EU and Turkey have strong interdependency, which is slowly turning towards the latter's benefit,[3] inequality in power does not mean that dialogue is not possible... inequality in power does not mean that dialogue is not possible. The question is what role each participant assumes in the negotiations.

The EU accession process is a bureaucratic exercise that is often misleadingly referred to as 'negotiations' and 'talks'. As Professor Marc Maresceau (2010), Professor of Law at Ghent University, points out, all that is negotiated between the EU and the candidate country is the timetable in which the EU imposed reforms will be carried out. As such, formal dialogue between the Union and a candidate state is a one-way system. When it comes to the formal modes of communication, a candidate country remains a passive participant, a silenced object. In concrete terms, it is the European Commission that engages in dialogue with the candidate country as stipulated by the rules concerning the enlargement process. Since 1998 the European Commission have published public annual regular reports on Turkey's progress towards accession. There is no corresponding public report on Turkey's side, which reduces Turkey into a silenced partner in the process.

The extent to which the utterances of Germany and France—the EU's most influential member states—against Turkey's membership are reflected in the Commission reports is difficult to evaluate, but the fear of a veto is certainly playing a role. The incumbent French and German leaders have continuously repeated their negative stance on Turkey's EU membership, advocating a special arrangement for Turkey. Claiming to represent the public view of his country, the French president Nicolas Sarkozy last reiterated his opposition to Turkey's membership during an official visit to Turkey in March 2011. The German Chancellor Angela Merkel made similar remarks during her official visit to Turkey a year before.

It is not only in the formal accession framework that Turkey is a non-answerable object. Turkey is silenced in other forums as well. One example is the Common Security and Defence Policy. As a NATO member since 1952 and with its second largest army, Turkey has actively contributed towards European security both during and after the Cold War. With its key geostrategic position, Turkey is pivotal to the EU. Prior to the creation of the European Security and Defence Policy (ESDP, later CSDP) in the Helsinki European Council in December 1999, the only active framework for handling specifically European security questions was the Western European Union (WEU) and the special partnership it held with NATO. Within this framework, Turkey—as an associate member—enjoyed a relatively strong status. As stated in the 1992 Petersberg Declaration of the WEU Council of Ministers, associate members

> *will have the same rights and responsibilities as the full members* for functions transferred to WEU from other fora and institutions to which they already belong; *they will have the right to speak* but may not block a decision that is the subject of consensus among the member states; they may associate themselves with the decisions taken by member states; they will be able to participate in their implementation unless a majority of the member states, or half of the member states including the Presidency, decide otherwise; they will take part on the same basis as full members in WEU military operations to which they commit forces; ... [and] they will be asked to make a financial contribution to the Organization's budgets. (WEU Council of Ministers, 1992, p. 10, own emphasis)

However, with the creation of the ESDP, Turkey's status was relegated. As Blockmans (2010, p. 8) states,

> in the WEU the associate members and partners participated in the regular Council of Ministers, but that would be unlikely in the General Affairs Council of the EU as the Treaty on European Union did not (and still does not) allow non-members to actively participate in regular council meetings. In fact, the Union has devised special bodies for meetings with other countries.

In essence, the logic had shifted from inclusion to exclusion, from being allowed to voice utterances to needing to keep silent. Turkey was no longer able to speak at meetings where important ESDP policies and operations were to be decided.

The EU also denied Turkey the previously existing provision of participating 'on the same basis as full members' in EU-led operations; excluded Turkey from the EU Military Staff (EUMS); took away Turkey's former status in the EU Institute; and disregarded Turkey's concern for the possibility that EU-led operations could take place in Turkey's own unstable neighbourhood and impact directly on its strategic interests. In Bakhtinian terms, the EU denied—despite its strong military and defence dependency on Turkey—the existence outside itself of another consciousness with equal rights and equal responsibilities. As a response, Turkey has been since blocking further development of EU–NATO co-operation. Some improvements have taken place, particularly in the EU's Copenhagen European Council of 12–13 December 2002 and the subsequent signing of the EU–NATO Declaration that opened the way for the detailed development of 'Berlin Plus'[4] arrangements. Still, one cannot speak of a strategic partnership between the EU and Turkey in the field of civil–military security co-operation.

A Dialogic Relationship

Why is Turkey's case any different from previous candidacies? All the candidate states have had to go through this monologic process. It is because Turkey's membership application is like no other in the past. Historically Europe has constructed its self-image vis-à-vis the Ottoman Empire, and vice versa. Europe ended where the Empire started. As Neumann (1999, pp. 39–40) argues,

> the dominant other in the history of the European state system remains 'the Turk', and because of the lingering importance of that system, we have here a particularly important other. In contrast to the communities of the New World, 'the Saracen' and 'the Ottoman' had the military might, the physical proximity, and a strong religious tradition that made it a particularly relevant other in the evolution of the fledgling international society that evolved from the ashes of Western Christendom and that took up a pivotal position in the forging of European identities.

Of course, since the dissolution of the Empire, Turkey has been moving towards the West and reinventing itself as a western state. As Neumann (1999, p. 60) continues:

> With the demise of the Ottoman empire in the wake of the 1908 revolution of the Young Turks and the defeat in World War I, a representation of Turkey began to take shape as a normalizing and modernizing nation and, with its entry into NATO, even as a trusted ally. More important, in being represented as a case of normalization, the transformation from a sick man to a reborn and young body politic also made 'the Turk' less central as a constitutive other.

Indeed, during the Cold War, Turkey anchored itself tightly in the western camp where it was considered a pivotal strategic ally. However, it was only in 1999 that Turkey was given a candidate status that materialised in 2005 with the accession process finally commencing.

Europe still needs Turkey to construct its self-identity. The past image of Turkey as *the ultimate other* carries through in the EU's current utterances towards Turkey. Turkey stands out from the other past and present accession states in attracting this sort of fundamental rejection; only Russia perhaps is comparable. Turkey's ability to not be able to answer back closes it in that image. It leaves it with no room for manoeuvre. But monologism, as Guillaume (2002, p. 9) argues, stands on an unsound ethical and epistemological position. In fact, as he continues,

> they tend to subvert the other, and do not allow it a proper conscience that is reflexively identical to them. Within a monological figuration, the other becomes an object of the self's own conscience, which can be interpreted and modified at will as a function of the self's own needs as an identity.

Paradoxically it is precisely the dialogic relationship that is needed for the EU to complete and perfect itself. As Guillaume (2002, p. 9), paraphrasing Bakhtin, points out: 'ethically, the completion and perfection of a self is determined by the reflexive and dialogical integration of otherness'.

The current situation between the EU and Turkey has led Turkey to 'anticipate the possible definition or evaluation others might make of him, to guess the sense and tone of that evaluation' and to try 'painstakingly to formulate these possible words about himself by others, interrupting his own speech with the imagined rejoinders of others' (Bakhtin, 1984, p. 52). As a candidate state, Turkey is subject to monologist utterances:

> In a monologic design, the hero is closed and his semantic boundaries strictly defined: he acts, experiences, thinks, and is conscious within the limits of what he is, that is, within the limits of his image as defined as reality; he cannot cease to be himself, that is, he cannot exceed the limits of his own character, typicality or temperament without violating the author's monologic design concerning him. Such an image is constructed in the objective authorial world, objective in relation to the hero's consciousness; the construction of that authorial world with its points of view and finalising definitions presupposes a fixed eternal position, a fixed authorial field of vision. The self-consciousness of the hero is inserted into this rigid framework, to which the hero has no access from within and which is part of the authorial consciousness defining and representing him—and is presented against the firm background of the external world. (Bakhtin, 1984, p. 52)

But consciousness of the self, as Bakhtin (1984, p. 53) writes, 'lives by its unfinalizability, by its closedness and its indeterminancy'. It is precisely the opposite—finalisability, closedness and determinancy—that the EU seeks to achieve with its membership talks. The only way Turkey can avoid this is to step away from the EU track. The problem lies in the authorial position of the EU. Rather than attempting to finalise and determine Turkey, the EU should adopt a *'fully realised and thoroughly consistent dialogic position*, one that affirms the independence, internal freedom, unfinalizibility, and indeterminacy of the hero'. (Bakhtin, 1984, p. 63)

Indeed, in the accession negotiations, Turkey should have a right to speak, to be able to answer back. Turkey should not be a mute, voiceless object of the author's words, but an answerable actor. Bakhtin (1984, p. 63) writes that 'only a dialogic and participatory orientation takes another person's discourse seriously, and is capable of approaching it both as a semantic position and as another point of view'. Turkey's ability to speak in the official accession framework would take EU–Turkey relations a step forward. Sevinc (2010, p. 98) writes that Turkey needs to 'implement a comprehensive communication strategy aiming at better informing the Turkish and the European publics of the conditions, obligations and advantages of EU's enlargement to Turkey'. This communication strategy should be institutionalised in the accession framework. For example, a report akin to the Commission's annual progress reports from Turkey's side would allow Turkey a voice. In that report Turkey could address the reforms it has undertaken during that year and issues of concern on the EU side. It could also provide its own rationale on the more thorny issues between the two sides, and reflect the current moods in the country.

As Nora Fisher Onar (2011, p. 43) writes, 'the task then is to reframe increasingly acrimonious relations in the name of mutual benefit which, in turn, may allow for both the recognition of commonalities and celebration of differences'. She proposes a 'gradual' or 'graduated' integration and membership; a model that has become increasingly popular option among policy analysts (see, for example, Karakas, 2006). Finland's Foreign Minister Alexander Stubb proposed in 2010 that the EU needs a dignified foreign policy based on listening, dialogue and mutual respect.[5] A more dialogic relationship between the EU and Turkey would be in line with his proposal that seeks to reverse 'the EU's declining influence in the world, where there are more competing actors, goals and values than in the past'.

Conclusion

In the EU accession process, the candidate country is a passive object. As such, the process does not differ from any usual process determining membership of a club. A candidate for membership is always put through a series of exercises to test his credentials. However, EU accession is a very particular process that has a significant impact on the candidate country's political system and society. This monologist, one-sided approach has created a deadlock in EU–Turkey accession process because the EU still defines itself through Turkey. Its self-image is intertwined with the image of Turkey as the ultimate other. The EU tries to rid itself of that image and create a union based on shared normative values. But it cannot do this without embarking on a genuine dialogue with Turkey.

In this situation, a dialogic relationship—one in which both sides are answerable participants—is a necessity. Without dialogism, the process has become an endeavour in which the EU has finalised and determined Turkey in the image of otherness vis-à-vis Europe. This deadlock can be broken only if Turkey is given a right to speak, to answer back, and to escape from the determined image. Institutionalising the right in the accession framework would be a solution to this. One possibility could be to establish an annual public report akin to the Commission's progress reports that a candidate state produces.

Notes

[1] Turkey in Europe: breaking the vicious circle, *Independent Commission on Turkey*, 7 September 2009.

[2] Xavier Guillaume (2002, p. 4) writes that:

> [s]ince the West discovered his work in the 1970s, Mikhail Bakhtin has been a major influence and source of renewal in many disciplines of the humanities, to the point that he unfortunately has become more and more an intellectual (and fashionable) icon, or even *cliché*, in the field.

[3] For example Finnish Foreign Minister Alexander Stubb argues that Turkey is 'more influential in the world than any of our member states together or separately' and 'one of the top five countries in the world today' (*Today's Zaman (online version)*, 'Finland's Stubb: "Turkey one of world's top five countries"', 13 September, 2010).

[4] Berlin Plus refers to the transfer of roles from WEU to the EU in NATO's Berlin Ministerial meeting, 3–4 June 1996.

[5] 'Stubb: Three 'commandments' for a new EU foreign policy', Press Release, 12 November 2010, *Finland's Permanent Representation to the European Union*.

References

Bakhtin, M. (1984) *Problems of Dostoevsky's Poetics*, ed. and trans. C. Emerson (Minneapolis, MN: University of Minnesota Press).

Bakhtin, M. (1986) The problem of speech genres, in: C. Emerson & M. Holquist (Eds) *Speech Genres and Other Late Essays*, trans. V. W. McGee (Austin, TX: University of Texas Press), pp. 60–101.

Bakhtin, M. (1990) Author and hero in aesthetic activity, in: C. Emerson & M. Holquist (Eds) *Art and Aswerability: Early Philosophical Essays by M.M. Bakhtin*, trans. and notes V. Liapunov (Austin, TX: Texas University Press), pp. 4–256.

Blockmans, S. (2010) Participation of Turkey in the EU's common security and defence policy: kingmaker or Trojan horse?, *Katholieke Universiteit Leuven*, Working Paper No. 41, March.

Bonnett, A. (2004) The Idea of the West: Culture, Politics and History (New York: Palgrave Macmillan).
Der Derian, J. & Shapiro, M. J. (Eds) (1989) *International/Intertextual Relations* (Lexington: Lexington Books).
Ellemann-Jensen, U. (2006, November 16) A fair deal for Turkey, *Project Syndicate*, http://www.project-syndicate.org/commentary/ellemann12/English (last accessed 8 January 2012).
Evin, A., Kirisci, K., Linden, R., Straubhaar, T., Tocci, N., Tolay, J. (2010) Getting to zero: Turkey, its neighbors and the West, *Transatlantic Academy*.
Fisher Onar, N. (2011) From inspiring to declining union, in: *What the EU Did Next: Short Essays for a Longer Life* (Berlin: Deutsche Gesellschaft für Auswärtigen Politik), pp. 40–44.
Guillaume, X. (2002) Foreign policy and the politics of alterity: a dialogical understanding of international relations, *Millennium*, 31(1), pp. 1–26.
Hürriyet Daily News (2010, July 7) NATO chief slams EU over 'unfair' Turkish treatment, *Hürriyet Daily News*.
Johansson-Nogues, E. & Jonasson, A.-K. (2011) Turkey, its changing national identity and EU accession: explaining the ups and downs in the Turkish democratization reforms, *Journal of Contemporary European Studies*, 19(1), pp. 113–132.
Journal of Turkish Weekly (2006, April 22) Ankara warns against 'unfair' EU conditions on Turkey, *Journal of Turkish Weekly*.
Karakas, C. (2006) Gradual integration: an attractive alternative integration process for Turkey and the EU, *European Foreign Affairs Review*, 11(3), pp. 311–331.
Maresceau, M. (2010) *Post-Cold War Experiences: Central Europe*. Lecture, European Union Institute for Security Studies Summer School, College of Europe, Warsaw, July.
Neumann, I. B. (1999) *Uses of the Other: 'The East' in European Identity Formation* (Minneapolis, MN: University of Minneapolis Press).
Sevinc, K. (2010) How to negotiate with the EU: theories and practice, *Turkish Policy Quarterly* 2010:96, pp. 95–99.
Today's Zaman (2010, September 13) Finland's Stubb: Turkey one of world's top five countries, *Today's Zaman*.
WEU Council of Ministers (1992) Bonn, Petersberg Declaration, 19 June.

Turkey's Path to EU Membership: An Historical Institutionalist Perspective

GULAY ICOZ*
Royal Holloway, UK

ABSTRACT *Scholars have drawn heavily on new institutionalist approaches in the study of comparative European politics and European integration. However, these approaches have been neglected in the study of Turkey–EU relations, resulting in a significant gap in the academic literature. In particular, the extant literature fails to question the significance of domestic political institutional settings and also fails to ask what role Turkey's National Security Council (MGK) played in shaping Turkey's path towards EU membership. The Historical Institutionalist approach, and the associated concepts of path dependence and punctuated equilibrium, can help address these failures by highlighting the importance of two significant phases of Turkey's European policy: the MGK's tendency to rule through states of emergency and its incompatibility with EU membership criteria (1983–1997); and the curtailment of the MGK's powers and the EU's decision to begin accession negotiations (1997–2004). To substantiate the value of historical institutionalism, I will first discuss the utility of the approach and justify its selection as a framework for explaining Turkey–EU relations. I will then discuss, in general terms, the ways in which institutions shape political action and maintain long periods of stasis. I will then demonstrate the utility of the concept of path dependence in researching the interaction between the MGK's use of state of emergency legislation and Turkey's path towards EU membership. The final part argues that the changes in the MGK and in Turkey–EU relations can be best understood with the historical institutionalist concept of punctuated equilibrium*

Scholars have drawn heavily on new institutionalist approaches in the study of comparative European politics (Przeworski, 1991; Rose & Davies, 1994; Hansen, 2002) and European integration (Pierson, 1996; Gorges, 2001; Meunier & McNamara, 2007). These approaches however have been neglected in the study of Turkey–European Union (EU) relations, resulting in a significant gap in the academic literature. In particular, the extant literature fails to question the significance of domestic political institutional settings and also fails to ask what role Turkey's National Security Council (MGK) played in shaping Turkey's path towards EU membership. The historical institutionalist approach, and the associated concepts of path dependence and punctuated equilibrium, can help address these failures by highlighting the importance of two significant phases of Turkey's European policy: the MGK's tendency to rule through states of emergency and its incompatibility with EC

(European Community)/EU membership criteria (1983–1997); and the curtailment of the MGK's powers and the EU's decision to begin accession negotiations (1997–2004). To substantiate the value of historical institutionalism, I will first discuss the utility of the approach and justify its selection as a framework for explaining Turkey–EU relations. I will then discuss, in general terms, the ways in which institutions shape political action and maintain long periods of stasis. Following this I will demonstrate the utility of the concept of path dependence in researching the interaction between the MGK's use of state of emergency legislation and Turkey's path towards EU membership. The final part argues that the changes in the MGK and in Turkey–EU relations can be best understood by the concept of punctuated equilibrium.

Turkey–EU relations have been widely researched (Calis, 2001; Onis, 2001; Lagro & Jorgensen, 2007; Faucompret & Konings, 2008), but the role of institutions in determining Turkey's relationship with the EU has been neglected. For example, Cayhan (1997) assessed Turkish political parties' stances on Turkey's European policy, but she overlooked the crucial fact that most parties have been inconsistent in their stances and did not consider how institutional arrangements in Turkish politics might have contributed to their inconsistency. Alternatively, Laciner *et al.* (2005, p. 14) examined Turkey's new role in world politics after the 11 September 2001 attacks in New York and the March 2004 Madrid bombings and concluded that 'probably only a Europe with Turkey may embrace the world ... there is no other alternative'. However, Laciner *et al.* did not recognise that Turkey's geo-strategic and geo-political importance to Europe has been overshadowed not only by the problematised domestic political dynamics, but also the nature of the decisions and policy preferences made by the political institutions in handling the internal matters.

More generally, there has been little scholarly engagement with the role of Turkey's National Security Council (MGK) in shaping the country's European policy. I will contribute to the literature on Turkey–EU relations by showing that the MGK played a significant role in Turkey–EC/EU relations between 1983 and 2004. This will be done by demonstrating both that Turkey's aspiration to join the EC/EU was always unlikely because of the MGK's repeated support for state of emergency rule (1983–1997), and that changes in the pace of Turkey–EU relations (1997–2004) were triggered by changes in the MGK.

New institutionalism emerged as a critique of the behavioural revolution in political science. While the other explanatory approaches, such as constructivism emphasises the importance of 'identity' to understand what shapes a state's foreign policy (Wendt, 1999), the new institutionalists argue that the institutions matter, and they seek to understand what role the institutions play in the determination of social and political outcomes (Hall & Taylor, 1996, p. 953). Hall and Taylor (1996, p. 936) identify three strands within the new institutionalism: rational choice institutionalism; sociological institutionalism; and historical institutionalism. All three might shed light on the importance of the MGK, but historical institutionalism is likely to be most useful. As Pierson and Skocpol (2002, p. 697) note, historical institutionalism tends to engage with big and real world questions of interest far beyond the academy. Questions like 'why have welfare states emerged and developed along various paths?' or 'why have some countries become stable democracies, while others have not?' constitute clear real world puzzles that are not driven by methodological or narrow theoretical concerns (Meunier & McNamara, 2007, p. 4). Likewise, I address the important puzzle of why Turkey has been waiting for so long to join the EU and question what developments in Turkey affected the prospects of membership between 1983 and 2004. A second reason why historical institutionalism can help shed light on the importance of the MGK is its emphasis on the importance of history and past policy choices in determining political action, or path dependence (Pierson & Skocpol, 2002, p. 713). By contrast, rational choice institutionalism treats history simply as a series of discrete events in which strategic actions are taken by utility maximising agents. Sociological institutionalism similarly does not pay much attention to the role of history; it suggests that individuals act in accordance with the expectations of the given cultural settings. I argue that both of these strands of new institutionalism underplay the role of history in the study of how institutions determine political actions. They therefore not only lack tools to trace history to unveil patterns and sequences of the decisions made in the past, but also overlook the relationship between the past and the future decisions or the choices institutions make. In addition, rational choice institutionalism's emphasis on strategic actions does not pay attention to the situations where an institution like the MGK opts to maintain its original path over a decade while neither the Turkish political system nor Turkey–EU relations benefited from this. A third reason to apply historical institutionalism is its inherent advantages compared with the other new institutionalist strands. Neither rational choice institutionalism's suggestion that institutions change when they are dysfunctional (Lecours, 2005, p. 12) nor sociological institutionalism's concept of isomorphism (Meyer & Rowan, 1977) provide a framework for questioning what precipitated the changes both in the MGK and in the pace of Turkey–EU relations. Historical institutionalism however points to the sources of change, for example exogenous crisis/shock (Krasner, 1984).

Path dependence is a simple concept. Sewell (1996, pp. 262–263) defines it as a relationship whereby 'what happened at an earlier point in time will affect the possible outcomes of a sequence of events occurring at a later point in time'. On the question of how and why institutions maintain their original path, I will adopt Pierson's perspective. Pierson (2004, p. 21) says that the paths, once created, are inflexible in the sense that further steps on a certain path make shifting from that path to another one much more difficult. The reason for this, according to Pierson (2000, p. 252), is a result of 'increasing returns'; the probability of further steps along the same path increases with each move down that path due to the relative benefits of the current activity compared with other possible options. However, the concept of path dependence has been criticised for blinding researchers to gradual changes (Gorges, 2001). The concept of path dependence will be defended by showing that Pierson's conceptualisation rigorously confirms the availability of other options to the institutions' original path. The researcher therefore is aware of the possibility that the institutions can drift away from their original path if they opt for one of the other options.

The concept of path dependence however does not adequately question whether the original paths always produce the intended outcome/s in the long term; I therefore propose to complement it with the concept of unintended consequences. Unintended consequences are central to historical institutionalism (Thelen, 1999) and it is agreed that institutions may not always produce the intended outcomes (Hall & Taylor, 1996, pp. 941–942). There are two important works by Pierson (1996) and Vachudova (2007) which employed this concept in different empirical case studies, but their analyses have not been discussed in the context of path dependence and the origins of the concept have been overlooked. I furthermore not only will contribute to the literature on how institutions shape policy outcomes through a framework that is based on both of the concepts of path dependence and the unintended consequences, but will also show that Robert K. Merton is one of the early scholars who named the concept of unintended consequences. Merton (1936, p. 895) said 'the consequences of purposive action are limited to those elements in the resulting situation which are exclusively the outcome of the action, i.e., those elements which would not have occurred had the action not taken place'. He also pointed to 'imperious immediacy of interest' as one of the sources of unintended consequences. Aydinonat (2008, pp. 14–15) explained this idea as an action that is taken to achieve an outcome without thinking about the other further consequences of this action.

As for institutional change, Krasner (1984, p. 240) refers to punctuated equilibrium as a notion which implies that the normal pattern of institutional equilibrium or stasis is punctuated by sudden changes caused by exogenous pressures. Krasner said, 'punctuated equilibrium is an apt description of an analytic stance that sees political institutions enduring over long periods once they are established' (1984, p. 243) and argued that the pressure for change tends to be exogenous, rather than endogenous. His conceptualisation is helpful because it provides a framework of questions—which will be outlined below—but I do not agree with Krasner that institutional changes tend to be underpinned by exogenous pressure. In this article, I will show that endogenous pressure also tends to trigger institutional changes; by endogenous pressure, I mean the pressure for change that is generated by the political developments in the areas the institution under study is responsible.

My emphasis on endogenous pressure furthermore will allow me to defend the use of concept of punctured equilibrium against Thelen and Steinmo (1992, p. 15) who said that at the moments of crisis institutions are dependent variables as their future is determined by the external political developments. Thelen and Steinmo's criticism is a fair one, but I will show later in this article that if the institution in question is changed by endogenous pressure, then it continues to be an independent variable. Another criticism of the concept of punctuated equilibrium came from Peters *et al.* (2005, p. 1289) who argued that there appears to be little or no capacity to predict occurrence of punctuations in a given stable path. I do not agree with Peters *et al.* and suggest that one may predict changes to occur both in the MGK's position in the Turkish political system and in Turkey–EU relations after many years of stasis.

Institutional Stasis—the MGK's Preference for a Path of State of Emergency and Turkey's Quest for EC/EU Membership (1983–1997)

The MGK gained a new position in the Turkish political system after the 1980 coup. Under Law 2945,[1] the MGK was asked to determine an opinion on the application of the national security policy of the Turkish Republic; national security in this context means the defence and protection of the State against all external and internal threat. The MGK defines internal threat as widespread acts of violence threatening the constitutional settings, indivisibility of the country and public order. In addition, Article 118 of the 1982 Constitution said the Council of Ministers shall give priority consideration to the decisions of the MGK. During the coup, the army adopted a pro-European stance. However, upon Kenan Evren's, the Chief of Staff and President of the State, decisions to abolish the Turkish Grand National Assembly (TBMM), suspend the Constitution and ban all political parties, the EC declined negotiations with Turkey over the Fourth Financial Protocol of the Association Agreement. Three years later, at the 1983 General elections, Turgut Ozal, the leader of Motherland Party (ANAP), was elected as the next Prime Minister. One of Ozal's political priorities was to re-establish regular political dialogue with the EC to revitalise Turkey–EC relations.

However, the emergence of the PKK and its venture to create a unified and independent Kurdistan, on the basis of its revolutionary Marxist–Leninist views, held back Ozal and successive governments from making progress in Turkey's bid to join the EC/EU. Cornell (2001, p. 31) suggests that the Kurdish question is the most serious domestic obstacle standing in the way of Turkey's bid for membership of the EU, and Van Bruinessen (2000, p. 28) argues that Turkey's poor performance in human rights and its handling of the Kurdish issue have been a big concern for the EU. However, neither scholar explains how and why the Kurdish issue has been such an obstacle. More importantly, neither explores how the MGK's handling of the PKK impacted on Turkey–EU relations. The historical institutionalist concept of path dependence is especially fruitful for such an endeavour.

The PKK's first attack was launched on military installations near Eruh and Semdinli in August 1984. This was followed by clashes between the Turkish Security Forces (TSK) and the PKK. Until 1985, these incidents were not reflected in the MGK's discussions, then the MGK referred to them as 'regional unsettlements',[2] and as 'terrorist movements'.[3] In the meantime, the MGK also gradually removed martial law from many parts of Turkey and replaced it by a state of emergency. By 1987, a state of emergency zone was settled in the ten Kurdish provinces: Batman; Bingol; Diyarbakir; Elazig; Hakkari; Mardin; Siirt; Sirnak; Tunceli; and Van.[4] This is where the PKK camps were located and the fight between the PKK militants and TSK soldiers generally took place. Legally, the MGK calls a state of emergency when 'there appears serious indications resulting from widespread acts of violence, which aimed at destroying the free democratic order of fundamental rights and freedom, or violent acts causing serious deterioration to public order' (Alexander et al., 2008, pp. 90–91). Whether the MGK's decision to keep the state of emergency in the ten Kurdish provinces influenced its subsequent recommendations to the Council of Ministers in how to handle the PKK, the MGK's press meeting releases[5] show that the MGK opted to re-extend the state of emergency every four months between 1987 and 1997.

Why did the MGK opt to maintain the state of emergency between 1987 and 1997; did the MGK's path of state of emergency generate benefits either to the Turkish political system or to Turkey's European policy, and if so, did these benefits increased over the years? Did the MGK have other options to its path of state of emergency? The following will answer these questions to show the interaction between the MGK's path of state of emergency and Turkey's aspirations to join the EC/EU. Then it will assess implications for the future of Turkey's European policy.

There are three important points to make. Firstly the MGK called a state of emergency to protect the indivisibility of Turkey, to safeguard constitutional settings and public order and to eradicate the PKK with its support base among local people. However, apart from protecting Turkey's territorial unity, the MGK did not achieve its other aims: the constitutional settings were not safe-guarded because the authority of the TBMM was undermined by the regional governors and village guards who ruled parts of the south-east of Turkey. The local people were left to conduct themselves in accordance with the requirements of the terrorism law. Furthermore, the MGK failed to eradicate the PKK, as it still exists today; and public order was not safeguarded as the local people and general public in Turkey still feel insecure because of constant clashes between the TSK and the PKK.

The second point is that the path of state of emergency did not have noticeable benefits to the Turkish political system. Under the state of emergency regime, businessmen were discouraged from making investments into the Kurdish region as there were constant military operations; locals were prevented from exercising their civil liberties and were restricted in their mobility and rights of assembly; and many of the schools in the region were shut, which deprived a significant proportion of school children of the opportunity to study. As a result, the Kurdish regions remained poor and underdeveloped. On the question why it received less economic and financial investments, Kirisci and Winrow (1997, p. 122) said 'it would be wrong to suggest that this was the product of deliberate policy on the part of the Turkish government'. In that case, one needs to ask what or which institution produced and perpetuated the level of impoverishment in the Kurdish region. Heper (2007, pp. 160–161) states that the situation in the Kurdish region was not 'the official policy of Ankara'. I agree with Heper that it was not an official policy, but one should not overlook the fact that the civilian and military members of the MGK have equal say on the decisions made in the MGK. I therefore argue that the MPs and some of the government ministers who sat on the MGK between 1983 and 1997 played an equal part in shaping the nature of the recommendations made by the MGK.

The third point is that the MGK's path of state of emergency and its consequences, initially at least, prevented Turkey from revitalising its relationship with the EC; the Joint Committee Meetings with the EC were delayed due to Turkey's lack of institutionalised democracy (*Official Journal of the European Communities* (OJEC), no. C172/128, 24 April 1984). The following four years were marked by Ozal's aspirations to form a political dialogue with the EC and him being turned down for either Turkey's treatment of the Kurdish prisoners or the Kurdish issue. In contrast, Necmettin Erbakan, the leader of the Welfare Party (RP) said 'Turkey did not have a place in the European Community' (*Milli Gazete* [newspaper], 15 December 1987), and proposed that Turkey should rather chose to lead the Islamic Common Market, when Ozal was planning to apply for full membership of the EC. The European Commission report of 1989 found Turkey eligible for membership, but offered it first the prospect of a customs union.

The end of the cold war in 1989 and the collapse of Soviet Union (SU) were significant developments in international politics and they underpinned speculations over whether Turkey was losing its geo-strategic importance to the EC. In addition to Turkey's aspiration to join the EC, developing close ties with the newly independent Turkic states of Central Asia appeared as another option. Although the Government did not change their stance on Turkey's European policy, the features of the state of emergency and the introduction of the Copenhagen criteria made it significantly difficult to revitalise the relationship. In 1991, the European Parliament (EP) asked Turkish authorities 'to stop the prosecution of the Kurdish population and halt the evacuation of the villages' (OJEC, no. C 106/120, 22 April 1991). When the Turkish government however interpreted this as violation of its national and parliamentary sovereignty, it called off the long awaited Joint Parliamentary Committee meeting with the EC, scheduled for 23–25 March 1992. In the meantime, the Maastricht Treaty (1992) established the EU and led to both single European currency and Common Foreign and Security Policy. Then Ocalan called for unilateral ceasefire in order to create the basis for a peaceful solution (*Cumhuriyet* [newspaper], 12 March 1993), but the MGK and Suleyman Demirel, the President, did not take notice of his option of ceasefire. Moving on from this point, the Copenhagen criteria introduced further conditions to the Turkish authorities to comply with before it could join the EU: stability of institutions guaranteeing democracy; the rule of law; human rights; and respect for and protection of minorities and the existence of a functioning market economy (Bulletin, EC 6-1993: 13). When Turkey felt closest to full EU membership after having established the customs union with the EU in 1995, on 19 September 1996 the EP decided to freeze the financial aid to Turkey due to protracted human rights violations. Furthermore, the Luxembourg Summit's decision not to include Turkey in the EU's enlargement of 2004 'was a watershed in Turkey's relations with the EU' (Rumford, 2001, p. 94), after which Mesut Yilmaz, the Prime Minister, opted to freeze political dialogue with the EU.

The above analysis showed that the MGK's state of emergency not only failed in its terms but also produced no benefits either to the Turkish political system or to Turkey–EC/EU relations. I now want to use Merton's concept of unintended consequences to highlight the relationship between the MGK's path and its unintended consequences. To do this I ask: had the MGK not opted for the state of emergency path, would the situation in the Kurdish region have developed as it did? The short answer: 'Probably unlikely.' The detailed answer is that had the state of emergency not been called for an initial four months and had it not been consistently extended every four months, then the situation would not have developed the undemocratic characteristics it did and it would have not stalled Turkey's integration to the EC/EU. There is therefore a clear connection between the MGK's path of state of emergency and Yilmaz's decision to freeze Turkey's political dialogue with the EU, after years of Ozal's efforts to revitalise talks with the EU.

Institutional Change—the Curtailment of the MGK's Powers and the EU's Decision to Begin Accession Negotiations (1997–2004)

Turkey did not begin political dialogue with the EU until it was granted a candidate membership status at the Helsinki Summit in 1999 and to this point of history, the EU authorities did not say much on the MGK's position in the Turkish political system. However, the European Commission's regular reports (1998–2004) paid considerable attention to the MGK and have asked Turkish authorities to change the MGK's composition, powers, functions and internal structure. Thereafter, the years between 1997 and 2004 have been significant in witnessing changes both in the MGK and in the pace of Turkey–EU relations. As to why the MGK was changed was debated by many scholars: the EU or the European Commission's Regular reports triggered the changes in the MGK (Cizre, 2003; Onis, 2003; Faucompret & Konings, 2008). I disagree with the idea that the European Commission's regular progress reports initiated the changes in the MGK. The regular reports, which may be regarded as exogenous pressure, have rather provided Turkish authorities with a roadmap to comply with the requirements of beginning accession negotiations with the EU. The above scholars have overlooked the role of domestic political dynamics in their interpretations of the changes in the MGK. I will rather consider the developments concerning Turkey's internal threats through relying on the tools of concept of punctuated equilibrium.

The MGK's path of state of emergency and the unintended consequences of this path are in the MGK's remit and they can be named as 'endogenous factors'. Another area can be added to these factors; the Welfare Party's (RP) success in gaining the largest number of seats in the TBMM in 1995 resulted in political discomfort in Turkey— it was feared that the RP's religiously associated activities and decisions might endanger the secular nature of the Turkish Republic and therefore, from the late 1990s, the RP was closely scrutinised by the MGK. The MGK's handling of the RP and the rise of political Islam can be recognised as another endogenous factor.

Krasner's emphasis on institutions maintaining stasis for long stretches of time is appropriate here because, as shown above, there were changes neither in the MGK's position nor in the pace of Turkey–EC relations between 1983 and 1997. Then changes suddenly began; the equilibrium was punctuated after nearly fourteen years. The first area concerns the changes to the MGK. In 2001, the number of civilian members of the MGK was increased from five to nine; and in the same year, the wording of Article 118 was changed, emphasising the advisory nature of the MGK, stressing its role in making recommendations, where now the Government was only required to 'evaluate' the recommendations rather than give 'priority consideration' (*Hurriyet* [newspaper], 29 December 2001). In 2003, the executive and supervisory powers of the General Secretariat of the MGK were abolished (Bayramoglu, 2004, pp. 110–111); furthermore, in 2004, its representatives withdrew their membership from the Council of Higher Education (YOK). The second involves the changes in the endogenous factors; state of emergency was gradually lifted from the ten Kurdish provinces by 2002 and the TBMM adopted a law on 'social reinsertion' in 2003 in order to foster social peace in the Kurdish region. The third area covers the changes in the pace of Turkey–EU relations. Upon granting Turkey a candidate membership status, the EU offered Ankara a pre-accession strategy, designed to support the reforms that were necessary in preparing Turkey for membership. At the Nice Summit in December 2000, the EU Council approved an Accession Partnership Document (AP) and in March 2001, Turkey presented its programme for adaptation of Acquis Communautaire for the National Programme of Turkey (OJEC, no. 24352). When Turkey fulfilled the requirements of bringing into force six pieces of legislation to enhance human rights, and after having signed the Adaptation Protocol, and extending its existing Association Agreement with the EU to all new member states, including the Republic of Cyprus, the EU opened accession negotiations in 2005.

I identified changes above in the three interconnected areas of Turkish politics and now want to ask what punctuated stasis in these three areas? What type of pressure—exogenous or endogenous—triggered these changes? The following will answer these questions to unveil the sources of the changes and show how and why the MGK remained an independent variable when the changes in question took place.

I do not agree with Krasner's emphasis on the exogenous pressure and it is also shown above that the EU's regular reports have only assisted the Turkish authorities to comply with the EU's standards. For that reason it is important to study the antecedents to the changes outlined above. I identified two important developments in the endogenous factors. When Erbakan was in power as the PM, he promoted Islamic revival in Turkey and started a debate regarding the introduction of Islamic Law. Thus, at the MGK's 28 February 1997 meeting he was asked to implement eighteen measures designed to check the growth of religious fundamentalism. He however never implemented these measures and in 1998, the Constitutional Court banned the RP and suspended Erbakan from politics for threatening Turkey's secular constitution. Furthermore, by the late 1998s Syria expelled Ocalan after the Turkish government threatened Syria with war. The PKK leader initially sought refuge in Rome in Italy, but was detained at the Greek embassy in Kenya on 16 February 1999.

Oran (2005, p. 35) suggested that Ocalan's trial and then his arrest allowed the Turkish governments to take rigorous steps to consolidate democracy. I agree that after Ocalan's capture a wide scale of political reforms were made in Turkey and this contributed positively to Turkey's path of EU membership. Oran however neither outlines what political reforms he is referring to nor questions if these reforms took place after long years of stability. Most importantly he does not explain how and why Ocalan's arrest contributed to Turkey's democratisation period. Furthermore, Akcapar (2007, p. 41) argued that an improved internal and external security environment emerged in Turkey when Ocalan was arrested and added that this helped Turkey to improve its relationship with the EU. She similarly does not explain how and why Ocalan's capture generated an internal security environment and in what ways this changed the pace of Turkey–EU relations. I argue that the closure of the RP and the ban on Erbakan's political involvement not only should be studied along the capture of Ocalan when one questions the sources of the political reforms in Turkey, but also needs to be treated as another crucial development in Turkish political dynamics that have contributed to the emergence of internal security environment in Turkey.

I suggest that when the leaders of these two internal threats were removed from Turkish politics, an improved security environment emerged in Turkey. There are two reasons for this. The first concerns Ocalan's adoption of a conciliatory approach during his trial and his decision to end the PKK's armed conflict. The second reason is that upon the closure of the RP, the Justice and Development Party (AKP) was established by the former RP Members of Parliament (MP) and on the contrary to the RP, it has adopted a moderately Islamic and pro-European approach. Since these developments mentioned are related to the MGK's policy responsibilities, I argue that the MGK remained as an independent variable while the changes in the MGK, in the endogenous factors and in Turkey–EU relations took place.

Conclusions

The current literature on Turkey–EC/EU relations did not utilise the new institutionalism, in particular the historical institutionalism strand; moreover the relative neglect of institutionalism created a significant gap in understanding either the role of domestic politics in why Turkey has been waiting for so long to join the EC/EU or which institution's position in the political system contributed to the wait. Therefore, students of Turkish politics failed ask what role the MGK has played in shaping Turkey's path towards EU membership. The historical institutionalist framework is beneficial to get an insight of two significant phases of Turkey–EC/EU relations (1983–2004). The historical institutionalist concept of path dependence is useful in highlighting the interaction between the MGK's state of emergency and Turkey's European policy (1983–1997), through which it was shown that the MGK's choice of keeping the state of emergency more than fourteen years hindered Turkey's progress towards EC/EU membership. Additionally, the concept of unintended consequences sheds a light on the link between the MGK's path of state of emergency, and Turkey's weak democracy and human rights records. It has also been helpful in understanding why the MGK kept the state of emergency even though its characteristic stalled Turkey's integration to the EC/EU. Furthermore, the source of the changes in the MGK and in the pace of Turkey–EU relations (1997–2004) has been questioned with the concept of punctuated equilibrium. Within this framework, the role of endogenous pressure in precipitating institutional change has been studied. I have unveiled the significant role of the closure of the RP and the capture of Ocalan in generating an improved security environment in Turkish politics, which allowed the MGK's powers to be curtailed and Turkey to be given a date to begin accession negotiations with the EU.

Notes

[1] For more information on the Law 2945, go to www.msb.gov.tr.
[2] MGK Press meeting releases, 25 January 1985.
[3] MGK Press meeting releases, 31 May 1985; 2 March 1986.
[4] MGK Press meeting releases, 16 May 1987.
[5] MGK Press meeting releases, 16 May 1987; 26 October 1989; 23 February 1990; 27 December 1991; 25 February 1992; 30 March 1993; 28 December 1994; 25 January 1995; 25 July 1996 and 28 February 1997.

References

Akcapar, B. (2007) *Turkey's New European Era Foreign Policy on the Road to EU Membership* (USA: Rowman and Littlefield Publishers).
Alexander, Y. B., Edgar, H., Krause, S. T. & Tutuncuoglu, S. (2008) *Turkey: Terrorism, Civil Rights, and the European Union* (London: Routledge).
Aydinonat, N. E. (2008) *The Invisible Hand in Economics: How Economists Explain Unintended Social Consequences* (USA/Canada: Routledge).
Bayramoglu, A. (2004) *Asker ve Siyaset* (The army and politics), in: A. Insel & A Bayramoglu (Eds) *Bir parti, Turkiye'de Ordu* (A class, a political party, the army in Turkey), pp. 59–118 (Istanbul: Birikim Yayinlari).
Calis, S. H. (2001) *Turkiye-Avrupa Birligi Iliskileri, Kimlik Arayisi, Politik Aktorler ve Degisim* (Turkey and the EU relations, search for identity, political actors and changing attitudes) (Ankara: Nobel Yayinlari).
Cayhan, E. (1997) *Dunden Bugune Turkiye ve Avrupa Birligi iliskileri ve Siyasal Partilerin Konuya bakisi* (From past to the present, the Turkish political parties' views on the relations with the EU) (Istanbul: Boyut Maatbacilik).
Cizre, U. S. (2003) Demythologyzing the national security concept: the case of Turkey, *Middle East Journal*, 57(2), pp. 213–229.
Cornell, S. E. (2001) The land of many crossroads: the Kurdish question and Turkish politics, *Orbis*, 45(1), pp. 31–46.
Faucompret, E. & Konings, J. (2008) *Turkish Accession to the EU: Satisfying the Copenhagen Criteria* (Oxon: Routledge).
Gorges, M. J. (2001) The new institutionalism and the study of the European Union: the case of the social dialogue, *West European Politics*, 24(4), pp. 152–168.
Hall, P. A. & Taylor, R. C. R. (1996) Political science and the three new institutionalisms, *Political Studies*, 44(5), pp. 936–957.
Hansen, R. (2002) Globalization, embedded realism, and path dependence, the other immigrants to Europe, *Comparative Political Studies*, 35(3), pp. 259–283.
Heper, M. (2007) *The State and Kurds in Turkey: The Question of Assimilation* (UK & New York: Palgrave Macmillan).
Kirisci, K. & Winrow, G. M. (1997) *The Kurdish Question and Turkey* (GB: Frank Cass).
Krasner, S. (1984) Approaches to the state: alternative conceptions and historical dynamics, *Comparative Politics*, 16(2), pp. 223–246.
Laciner, S., Ozcan, M. & Bal, I. (Eds) (2005) *European Union with Turkey: The Possible Impact of Turkey's Membership on the European Union* (Ankara: International Strategic Research Organization Publications).
Lagro, E. & Jorgensen, K. E. (2007) *Turkey and the European Union: Prospects for a Difficult Encounter* (London: Palgrave).
Lecours, A. (2005) *New Institutionalism: Theory and Analysis* (Canada: University of Toronto Press).
Liebowitz, S. J. & Margolis, S. E. (1990) The fable of the keys, *Journal of Law and Economics*, 33(1), pp. 1–25.
Merton, R. (1936) The unanticipated consequences of human action, *American Sociological Review*, 1(6), pp. 894–904.
Meunier, S. & McNamara, K. R. (2007) *The state of the European Union: European integration and institutional change at fifty* (Oxford: Oxford Press).
Meyer, J. & Rowan, B. (1977) Institutionalizing organizations: formal structure as myth and ceremony, *American Journal of Sociology*, 83(2), pp. 340–363.
Onis, Z. (2001) An awkward partnership: Turkey's relations with the European Union in comparative-historical perspective, *Journal of European Integration History*, 7(1), pp. 105–119.

Onis, Z. (2003) Domestic politics, international norms and challenges to the state: Turkey–EU relations in the post-Helsinki era, in: A. Carkoglu & B. Rubin (Eds) *Turkey and the European Union, Domestic Politics, Economic Integration and International Dynamic*, pp. 8–31 (GB: Frank Cass).

Oran, B. (2005) *Turk Dis Politikasi Kurtulus Savasindan Bugune Olgular,* Belgeler, Yorumlar (Turkish foreign policy) (Istanbul: Iletisim yayinlari).

Peters, B. G., Pierre, J. & Kings, D. S. (2005) The politics of path dependence: political conflict in historical institutionalism, *Journal of Politics*, 67(4), pp. 1275–1300.

Pierson, P. (1996) The path to European integration: a historical institutionalist analysis, *Comparative Political Studies*, 29(2), pp. 123–163.

Pierson, P. (2000) Increasing returns, path dependence, and study of politics, *American Political Science Review*, 94(2), pp. 251–267.

Pierson, P. (2004) *Politics in Time: History Institutions and Social Analysis* (Princeton, NJ: Princeton University Press).

Pierson, P. & Skocpol, T. (2002) Historical institutionalism in contemporary political science, in: I. Katznelson & H. V. Milner (Eds) *Political Science, State of the Discipline*, pp. 693–721 (USA: W.W. Norton & Company).

Przeworski, A. (1991) *Democracy and the Market: Political and Economic Reforms in Eastern Europe and Latin America* (Cambridge: Cambridge University Press).

Rose, R. & Davies, P. (1994) *Inheritance in Public Policy* (New York: Oxford University Press).

Rumford, C. (2001) Human rights and democratization in Turkey in the context of EU candidature, *Journal of European Area Studies*, 9(1), pp. 93–105.

Sewell, W. H. (1996) Three temporalities: toward an eventful sociology, in: T. J. McDonald & A. Arbor (Eds) *The Historic Turn in the Human Sciences*, pp. 245–280 (Michigan: The University of Michigan Press).

Thelen, K. (1999) Historical institutionalism in comparative politics, *Annual Review of Political Science*, 2, pp. 369–404.

Thelen, K. & Steinmo, S. (1992) Historical institutionalism in comparative politics, in: S. Steinmo, K. Thelen & F. Longstreth (Eds) *Structuring Politics: Historical Institutionalism in Comparative Analysis*, pp. 1–32 (Cambridge: Cambridge University Press).

Vachudova, M. A. (2007) Historical institutionalism and the EU's eastward enlargement, in: S. Meunier & K. R. McNamara (Eds) *The State of the European Union European Integration and Institutional Change at Fifty*, pp. 105–122 (Oxford: Oxford Press).

Van Bruinessen, M. (2000) Transnational aspects of the Kurdish question, European University Institute (EUI), Working Papers.

Wendt, A. (1999) *Social Theory of International Politics* (Cambridge: Cambridge University Press).

Kurdish Transnational Politics and Turkey's Changing Kurdish Policy: The Journey of Kurdish Broadcasting from Europe to Turkey

BILGIN AYATA*
Research Group 'The Transformative Power of Europe', Freie Universität Berlin

ABSTRACT *The bulk of scholarship on EU–Turkey relations has focused mainly on intergovermental or state–society relations, while the larger literature on enlargement and Europeanization has hardly paid any attention to the role of diasporas and immigrant communities as relevant political entrepreneurs in Europeanization processes. In this article, I examine the role and impact of the Kurdish diaspora and the transnational politics of Kurds on recent policy changes in Turkey, with respect to Kurdish broadcasting. Until 1990, the Turkish state officially denied the very existence of Kurds, today Turkish state television broadcasts programs in the Kurdish language. Other reforms have taken place as well. This has often been explained as a result of EU conditionality, yet, no studies have explored the fact that all of these different aspects of Kurdish cultural and educational activities that have begun to take shape in Turkey were actually first developed and implemented in Europe, by Kurdish organizations themselves. The analysis of ROJ-TV in Europe shows that this Kurdish satellite channel is a paradigmatic example of how 'the diaspora strikes back'. I argue that the emergence of a state-sponsored Kurdish channel in Turkey is a further reaction by the Government to the existence of ROJ-TV in Europe, after initial efforts to shut down the station failed. I conclude that for a comprehensive understanding of Turkey's reform process the transnational activism of the Kurdish diaspora has to be taken into account.*

For more than three decades, one of Turkey's most pressing and unresolved problems has been the Kurdish conflict which has resulted in a massive forced displacement of at least one million Kurdish civilians, an estimated 44,000 killings of PKK (*Partiya Karkerên Kurdistan*—Kurdistan's Workers Party) militants, soldiers, and civilians, as well as grave human rights violations (HRW 2010). However, compared to the period before the 1990s, when the Turkish state vehemently suppressed any expression of a Kurdish culture and identity and even denied the very existence of Kurds (McDowall, 2005), the picture today looks rather different. Following the armed struggle of the PKK and the Kurdish mobilization, the Kurdish conflict has been on the top agenda of Turkish domestic politics leading to a gradual change of the previous official stance: in 1991, Prime Minister

Demirel had declared that Turkey recognizes its 'Kurdish reality'; in 1993, President Özal had even indicated the possibility for a political settlement with the PKK (Barkey & Fuller, 1998; Kirisci & Winrow, 1997). In the run up to gain candidacy status for EU membership, several reform packages were passed from 1999 onwards, that led to further liberalization regarding the expression of Kurdish culture and identity.

Arguably, however, the most symbolic break with previous denial policies occurred on 1 January 2009, when Prime Minister Erdogan inaugurated the 24-hour channel of the Turkish state television TRT that broadcasts daily programs in the Kurdish language and concluded his statement by uttering a sentence in Kurdish (*'TRT Şeş bi xêr be'*—May TRT 6 be auspicious). Given that earlier even the existence of a Kurdish language was denied, this indeed constitutes an historic moment in Turkey's official approach to the Kurdish issue. Back in 1991, the Kurdish MP Leyla Zana was banned from Parliament after she had spoken Kurdish during the oath ceremony, yet now, the Prime Minister himself uttered a Kurdish sentence on Turkish state television.

Moreover, in the course of the AKP (*Adalet ve Kalkinma Partisi*—Justice and Development Party) government's 'Democratic Initiative Process' launched in August 2009—which was later renamed 'National Unity and Fraternity Project'—Erdogan announced further reforms concerning Kurdish rights, including the establishment of Kurdish studies in two universities. Legal restrictions on publishing in Kurdish had already been lifted earlier. At present, Kurdish political actors such as the BDP (*Baris ve Demokrasi Partisi*—Peace and Democracy Party) are pushing the issue of primary education in the Kurdish language and it is now possible to learn Kurdish in private language courses and some universities. Even though the implementation of all these reforms is severely lagging behind and positive developments are often accompanied by new restrictions in other realms such as the detention of over 2,000 Kurdish politicians and activists since December 2009, they still pose a groundbreaking improvement when compared with the previous state policy of denial and persecution of Kurds in the Turkish Republic that reigned until the 1990s.

Scholars have commonly analyzed this remarkable shift in human rights and democratization in Turkish politics as a result of EU conditionality (Hale, 2003; Önis, 2003; Schimmelfennig *et al.*, 2003; Kubicek, 2005). Yet, no studies have acknowledged or explored the fact that all of these different aspects of Kurdish cultural and educational activities that have begun to take shape in Turkey were actually first developed and implemented in Europe by Kurdish organizations themselves. Especially regarding the issue of broadcasting in Kurdish, which has been the focus of much fervent discussion in the Turkish public and parliament, I argue that the emergence of a state-sponsored Kurdish channel in Turkey is a further reaction by the Government to the existence of the Kurdish satellite TV Station ROJ-TV in Europe, after the Turkish state's efforts to shut down the station failed. Up to now, the bulk of scholarship regarding EU-Turkey relations has focused by and large on intergovernmental relations or domestic state–society relations, while the larger literature on enlargement and Europeanization has hardly paid any attention on the role of diasporas and immigrant communities as relevant political entrepreneurs in Europeanization processes. In this article, I will examine the role and impact of the Kurdish diaspora and the transnational politics of Kurds on recent policy changes in Turkey, particularly with regard to Kurdish broadcasting.

Kurdish Transnational Activism in the European Diaspora

Given the restrictive political conditions for Kurds in their respective countries, politics in exile has become an important characteristic of Kurdish mobilization. Already in 1956, the first Kurdish organization in Germany was formed—'The Kurdish Students Society in Europe' (KSSE)—that became in the 1960s and 1970s an important forum for Kurdish politics in the Middle East (Van Bruinessen, 2000). In the course of the labor recruitment in the 1960s and 1970s large numbers of Kurdish migrants arrived in Europe which was added by the latest wave of migration in the 1990s, when thousands of Kurdish refugees fled to European member states in the course of the armed clashes in the Kurdish region in Turkey. The recent Kurdish displacement to Europe has resulted in a range of transnational mobilization efforts—with activities often directed toward 'home'—that have created a vibrant diaspora in Europe. This mobilization also included the Kurdish labor migrants who were already present in Europe. Prior to the 1990s, however, only small numbers of these labor migrants were involved in Kurdish activism and they were mostly subsumed under the category of Turkish immigrants in Europe. While there are no official numbers available it is generally estimated that about 1–1.5 million Kurds are living in Europe (Ember *et al.*, 2004). I have elsewhere conceptualized the myriad institutions and activities of this diaspora as 'Euro-Kurdistan'—not to be understood as a bounded geographical space, but rather, as a dynamic process of Kurdish collective-identity formation *in* and *through* Europe (Ayata, 2008, 2011). I argue in the present article that the transnational activities of the Kurdish diaspora have boomeranged back to Turkey both in terms of *social remittances* (targeting Kurdish political parties and Kurdish civil society), and also in terms of *political leverage*, putting the Turkish government under considerable pressure regarding its Kurdish policies.[1] The context of Turkey's EU candidacy has been an important factor in the development of Kurdish transnational politics and European norms and values frequently appear as a critical reference point in their claim-making and challenging of government policies in Turkey. Yet in order to assess the policy changes with regard to the Kurdish issue in recent years, we need to go beyond explanations limited to EU conditionality. In what follows, I will pursue this argument with the example of Kurdish broadcasting through a case study of the Kurdish satellite TV Station ROJ-TV.[2]

The case of Kurdish satellite TV in Europe provides an important illustration of how Kurdish transnational politics in the diaspora are effective means to counter some of the most resilient taboos and policies in Turkey. Not only have these Kurdish transnational activities of Kurdish organizations in Europe challenged Turkey from without, they have also contributed to substantial policy changes within Turkey. The example of ROJ-TV is a challenging and controversial one, due to its obvious affinities with the outlawed PKK, on the one hand, and its progressive, multilingual, multiculturalist programming that is in accordance with European norms and policies such as minority rights. Both ROJ-TV and activities of other organizations such as the Kurdish Human Rights Project (KHRP) have had important effects on political developments in Turkey, although through different transnational practices. Broadly speaking, while the activities of ROJ-TV relate to collective identity building (and maintenance) within the larger Kurdish community, other organizations such as those of the KHRP relate to awareness-raising and lobbying in Europe for the human rights of Kurds through rights-seeking in Europe (Ayata, 2011).

Immigrant Media as the Ear and Voice of Diasporas

Recent research on media consumption in Europe suggests that people with an ethnic minority background watch more television from their countries of origin than from the national TV channels of their host countries (Christiansen, 2004). In his study of news consumption among Swedish immigrants, Roald has even described satellite dishes as 'the immigrants' ear to the homeland' (cited in Christiansen, 2004, p. 186). Yet, migrant media are not just an ear to a distant homeland, but often 'the starkest examples of "voices" that express their dissent even after the exit from a nation-state' (Kosnick, 2008, p. 4). This is certainly the case for ROJ-TV, which is not just a diaspora TV station, but was—when founded as MED-TV in 1995—actually the first-ever TV station broadcasting in the Kurdish language to over 30 million Kurds in the Middle East. The only previous Kurdish-language broadcast existed in the former Soviet Union, when Radio Yerevan produced a short daily radio show in Kurdish from 1955 onwards. Therefore, the inauguration of a Kurdish TV station in 1995 represented a milestone within Kurdish politics, and Kurdish history in general.

Scholars of Kurdish nationalism have asserted that ROJ-TV, by reaching Kurdish viewers via satellite from Europe to the Middle East and Asia, has had a major impact not only on the standardization of the Kurdish language, but also on processes of Kurdish identity formation and nation-building (Hassanpour, 1998; Romano, 2006). Today, ROJ-TV broadcasts in seventy countries around the world via satellite, reaching Jewish Kurds in Israel as well as Kurdish refugees in Australia and Japan. Turkey wants European Memberstates to close down the station as it regards it as a propaganda outlet of the PKK, financed by illegal transactions of the outlawed organization. The producers of ROJ-TV claim that the station is financed through donations of Kurdish immigrants in Europe and that the Turkish government simply wants to prevent Kurdish broadcasting from outside of Turkey, just as it does within Turkey.[3]

Challenging Turkey from Europe through Satellite Television

That some of the programs of ROJ-TV are in the Kurdish language is only one of the problems the station presents for the Turkish state; arguably more important is the fact that this broadcasting occurs outside of Turkish state control and jurisdiction, and thus it could (and continuously does) provide news and opinions about the Kurdish conflict uncensored by Turkish authorities. The Turkish state has focused its critique on the frequent and visible presence of the PKK and its ideology in the station's broadcasting, but arguably the more damaging impact of the station has been its rupture of the Turkish military's monopoly of information regarding the internal war in the Kurdish region. By highlighting the suffering of Kurdish civilians, the station has fundamentally undermined the language of terrorism employed since 1990 by the Turkish state and the mainstream media, and provided the first unrestricted public counter-discourse. Preceding the Kurdish TV station in Europe was the experience of the pro-Kurdish daily *Özgür Gündem* that was first published in May 1992 in Turkey, which was met with violent reactions by the Turkish authorities. Only within the first two years of its publication, twenty-seven reporters and staff members of the newspaper were murdered by paramilitary forces; its offices were raided and its distribution obstructed (Aydemir, 2011). Even though the newspaper continued to be published later on, the experience with *Özgür Gündem* showed that while there was a demand for an alternative news source among the Kurdish population reporting about the internal war in the Kurdish region, it was extremely difficult to do so from within Turkey.

Unlike its Turkish media counterparts, ROJ-TV has not relied on military briefings as its sole source of information; instead, regarding the Kurdish conflict, the main source has been the PKK, with its key leaders and militants participating via phone from the mountains or training camps. More importantly, it was also the only TV station that reported constantly about the destruction of Kurdish villages and Turkey's depopulation policy in the Kurdish region at a time when the mainstream media in Turkey was completely silent on these issues.[4] Hence, the founding of the first Kurdish TV-station was not simply a cultural activity, but a profoundly political action that not only facilitated Kurdish mobilization in Europe and in Turkey, but also challenged the Turkish state in unprecedented ways. In addition to the military battle in the Kurdish mountains with weapons, the State was facing now a new challenge carried out on airwaves from TV studios in Europe reaching Kurdish households in Turkey.[5]

This challenge cannot be overstated considering that the Turkish media had put themselves overwhelmingly in the service of the Turkish military during the internal war. In his book, *The Kurds*, one of Turkey's most prominent journalists Hasan Cemal (2003) describes how in April 1990, all leading newspaper owners were called into the President's office, where President Özal and high-ranking military and secret service representatives gave them orders how *not* to report about what was going on in south-east Turkey. Some newspapers had earlier referred to the PKK as guerilla and described the Kurdish uprising as an intifada, which had enraged the military. In this meeting, the country's leading media owners were given clear instructions not to use such terms, and to report instead on dying soldiers as martyrs and only to report the events as instances of terrorism (Cemal, 2003, pp. 101–111). In fact, the language of terrorism was a central component in Turkey's counter-guerrilla strategy and was subsequently implemented and followed overwhelmingly by the Turkish media.

Hence without the news reporting of ROJ-TV that offered radically different news than Turkish media outlets, there would have been no collective knowledge about the scope of destruction and violence even among Kurds themselves, for instance that the village evacuations occurred on a systematic level. On ROJ-TV, the village destructions were primetime news for years on a daily basis, alongside coverage of torture, extrajudicial killings and human rights abuses against Kurds. It could be said that ROJ-TV's collective identity-building was based on a heightened notion of Kurdish victimhood at the hands of the Turkish state, and the inaction of the surrounding nation-states. By not presenting Kurds as 'better' or 'different' in terms of a racial discourse, and by focusing its critique on the Turkish state rather than on 'Turks' more generally, the programming content of ROJ-TV highlighted the victimization of Kurds by state violence and assimilation policies, while simultaneously stressing the plurality of cultures in the Middle East. This may be one important reason why the bloody armed conflict between the PKK and the Turkish military did not escalate into a civil war between Kurdish and Turkish civilians, as it did in the Balkans.

Evading State Power through Transnationalism

ROJ-TV began airing in March 1995 with a test transmission from London, back then under the name MED-TV. The reaction among the Kurdish population was enthusiastic, as this was the very first time in Kurdish history that a Kurdish TV station, owned and operated by Kurds themselves, was inaugurated. Less enthusiastic was the Turkish government, which took immediate action. As Kosnick (2008) elaborates in her analysis of MED-TV, before the station's first broadcast, the Turkish government had already pressured telecommunication companies not to provide a transponder, warning that the PKK was behind the channel. But the Turkish government not only tried to prevent the station from broadcasting, it also attempted to prevent viewers in Turkey from watching it through a number of various measures, such as jamming signals or destroying satellite dishes (Kosnick, 2008, p. 8).

In an effort to evade the reach of the Turkish state, the station was, from the beginning, a transnational undertaking. The main studios were set up in Belgium, but some programs were produced in Sweden and Germany. The license and the transponder had been obtained from several countries. When the diplomatic efforts of the Turkish state bore fruit in 1999 and MED-TV's broadcasting license was revoked by the UK, a new station was set up within several months in France, this time with the name MEDYA-TV. Then, in 2004, when MEDYA-TV's license from France was also revoked, ROJ-TV was founded in the same year, with a broadcasting license from Denmark. Since 2004, the Turkish government has prepared over twenty files on the station and sent them to the Danish authorities, demanding the closure of the station becuase of its alleged links with the PKK.[6] The current station director Yilmaz Imdat denies having financial and organizational links with the PKK and argues that their broadcast falls within the limits of freedom of expression in Europe.[7]

The fact that ROJ-TV receives its license from Denmark has led to repeated diplomatic tension between Turkey and Denmark, a relationship that has been strained since the cartoon crisis in 2005.[8] In 2006 the Turkish embassy in Copenhagen opened legal charges against ROJ-TV for allegedly maintaining links with a terrorist organization and inciting hatred. In protest, over fifty Kurdish mayors from Turkey sent Prime Minister Rasmussen a petition in support of ROJ-TV, calling for its continued permission to operate in Denmark.[9] These mayors were subsequently prosecuted in Turkey for sending this petition, which Rasmussen publicly criticized again with reference to European values of democracy and freedom of expression. A Danish court rejected the charges of the Turkish embassy in 2006. However, the issue of ROJ-TV emerged once again on the Turkish political agenda when the former Danish Prime Minister Rasmussen ran for Secretary General of NATO in 2008, with his election dependent on Turkey's vote. Turkey reiterated its demand for ROJ-TV to be closed down by Denmark and blocked the Danish Prime Minister's election until a concession regarding ROJ-TV was obtained.[10] In the meantime, Germany prohibited the station from broadcasting therein in 2008, but a court decision in April 2009 temporarily revoked this prohibition. The future of ROJ-TV remains uncertain and continues to burden Turkey's relationship with EU member states. It also continues to pose a challenge for Europe's relationship with its immigrants and its proclaimed values of multiculturalism and democratic liberties.

Diffusing European Norms through Kurdish Media?

Despite Turkey's pressure on EU member states to close the station, in my interviews with the ROJ-TV's former director of programming Ferda Cetin was rather confident about the future of the channel.[11] When I asked him how long the station could withstand the pressure, he responded with a counter question: 'Why should Europe close down our station? After all, everything that we do here is part and parcel of European norms!'[12] He argues that their vision for the Middle East stems directly from the reality of Europe, a vision where different cultures and nations live respectfully with their differences in a multicultural setting. In the station's self-understanding, ROJ-TV's programming principles already implement many European norms and values. Indeed, ROJ-TV offers programming not only in the four Kurdish dialects (Kurmanji, Sorani, Zazaki, Hamravi), but also broadcasts daily news in Turkish, Arabic, Farsi, and in English. In addition, they produce weekly programs for religious minorities such as for Alevis, Yezidis, and Assyrians. Once a week, ROJ-TV broadcasts a news show from the European Parliament, during which European MPs are introduced and the latest European developments reported.

According to Cetin, the mission of ROJ-TV is to nourish and cultivate the plurality and multiculturalism that exists both within the Kurdish community, as well as in its neighboring regions: 'On the one hand, yes, our programming principles take a Kurdish national identity as its base, not by suppressing or ignoring cultural plurality, but by emphasizing this as a positive, worthwhile aspect.' With this vision and practice, Cetin locates the Kurdish TV station closer to the European Union than to Turkey, and regards European norms as directly reflected in the fact that the station produced shows and news programs in several languages, and provides a forum for different cultures in Kurdistan and the Middle East. 'What do our Kurdish viewers in Iraq, in Turkey, in Iran see when they watch daily our programs? That our demands for cultural rights have to be extended to others as well, that we need to respect religious differences, and that democracy begins at our doorstep. This is nothing that can be said of Turkish or Iranian TV stations, and Europe knows that', argues Cetin. 'In a way, we are disseminating European norms such as multiculturalism, tolerance, equal rights, women's rights, etc., to our audience, not for strategic reasons, but because we believe in them'.

When I ask Cetin about the allegations of the Turkish state, that ROJ-TV incites hatred, maintains close links with the PKK and instigates Kurdish uprisings, he refers to the decisions of different European courts that have rejected these charges. In his view, Turkey's concern with the station stems not only from the fact that a Kurdish broadcast occurs outside of Turkey's control, but more specifically, from the fact that ROJ-TV's news programming reports extensively on issues such as the village evacuations and extrajudicial killings in south-east Turkey, while media within Turkey are strictly censored regarding these topics. Cetin argues that like those at ROJ-TV, the Turkish government understands that *'television is more powerful than weapons'*—a realization the producers of the station gained very quickly after its first transmissions in 1995. Not only was there a wide reception by Kurds who saw themselves represented and talked about as 'Kurds' for the first time on TV, but they also took notice of the strong negative reaction by the Turkish state. This, according to Cetin, made the producers realize that civil action, and especially the use of mass media is very effective both to advance a Kurdish nationhood and collective identity, and to counter Turkey's military might regarding the Kurdish issue.

Critics of the station have voiced doubts about how much of the emphasis on European norms is mere rhetoric to maintain the station in the face of ongoing pressure on European states to close it. Sedat Laciner (2010, p. 28), a prominent expert on terrorism and strategic studies in Turkey, argues that ROJ-TV only broadcasts programs on different religions and Christian Kurds in order to win sympathy among Christians in Europe. For him, as well as for many other critics of the station, it is the partisan politics of ROJ-TV toward the PKK that matter. Such concerns about the ulterior motivations of the station notwithstanding, the fact remains that ROJ-TV produces multilingual, multicultural shows, with progressive messages toward women's emancipation, democratic rights, tolerance, and religious freedom that reach Kurdish households both in Europe and in the Middle East.

Turkey's EU Candidacy and Kurdish Broadcast in Turkey after ROJ-TV

Since the founding of ROJ-TV, there have been various discussions both in the Turkish parliament and in the Turkish media whether Kurdish broadcasting should be permitted in Turkey, mostly in combination with debates regarding Turkey's quest for EU membership. In 1993, the EU adopted the Copenhagen Criteria for countries seeking accession for EU membership. Subsequently in December 2002, the European Council decided that if Turkey met the Copenhagen Criteria by 2004, the EU would open accession negotiations. Already in 2002, the Turkish parliament had declared that the bans on Kurdish education and broadcasting were to be lifted insofar as they did not threaten the indivisible territorial integrity of the Turkish state. During 2002 and 2004, public debate on minority rights, the Kurdish conflict, and democratic reforms ranked at the top of Turkey's political agenda and several reforms regarding minority protection were passed by the AKP government. In the course of these reforms, private language schools were legally permitted to offer Kurdish language courses and private TV stations were allowed to broadcast in Kurdish. Yet the actual implementation of these new possibilities for minorities has been hampered by administrative and bureaucratic interventions by local authorities, particularly when Kurds themselves have indicated a desire to open schools or TV stations (MRG, 2007, pp. 16–18). It seems that the new policy of the Government is to allow for liberalization and opening only as long as the State retains direct control, while initiatives and projects that come from minorities themselves, particularly by Kurdish actors, are still subject to an obstructive level of suspicion and suppression.

This ambiguous liberalization that has been progressing under the AKP government is best illustrated in a development that represents, in many ways, a historic moment for Turkey. While Turkey's efforts to shut down ROJ-TV have continued to intensify, the Government introduced in January 2009 a twenty-four-hour broadcast in the Kurdish language at the Turkish State Television (TRT). TRT has been a key institution in the maintenance of the Turkish nation-state along the official state ideology of Kemalism. A nationwide Kurdish broadcast on state television is, thus, an unprecedented step for the Turkish state with regard to its Kurdish population.[13] It thereby responds to a central demand by the Kurdish movement for cultural and political rights. But while Turkey's accession efforts for EU candidacy have certainly facilitated this step, I argue that the state television's Kurdish broadcast has to be evaluated in the context of the Turkish state's simultaneous effort to close down ROJ-TV. Rather than fighting ROJ-TV by diplomatic means only—which has proved largely unsuccessful for the past fifteen years—the Turkish state has now entered into a *competition* with ROJ-TV through TRT 6. Indeed, some politicians in Turkey had long argued that the best way to counter ROJ-TV was by offering an alternative Kurdish channel in Turkey (Laciner, 2010). The journalist Amberin Zaman (2009) aptly described the Government's new broadcasting policy with TRT 6 as 'battles shifting to airwaves'.

It is, indeed, a battle as ROJ-TV for its own part has been vehemently fighting TRT 6. The station regards TRT 6 as a deceptive move by the State to, paradoxically, assimilate the Kurds by using the Kurdish language—a concern that is also reflected by Kurdish politicians such as Atalay and Kisanak.[14] Kurdish musicians who agreed to do programs for TRT 6 were branded as traitors to the Kurdish people in ROJ-TV programs and the producers of TRT 6 had difficulties in recruiting Kurdish native speakers for the making of TRT 6 (Aytac, 2010). Apart from a few talk shows produced for TRT 6 only, most of the programming consists of translations from other TRT programming into Kurdish. Even pro-government observers such as Önder Aytac (2010, p. 111) conclude in a recent assessment of TRT 6, that 'the language used in TRT-6 is inadequate and the programs are dull content-wise. Showing ancient soap operas and Turkish films that are badly translated (into Kurdish) cannot be counted as professional televising.' Members of the BDP argue that the AKP only pushed TRT 6 through in order to increase its votes in the Kurdish regions, during the municipal elections in March 2009 (Zaman, 2009). Since the parliamentary elections in 2007, which the AKP won in a landslide, the only serious competitor for the AKP in the south-east has been the BDP, which has strongholds in Diyarbakir and other major Kurdish cities. This became even clearer in the 2011 elections, when the BDP increased its vote further in the Kurdish region. Yet irrespective of the possible electoral calculations by the AKP government, which has indeed entered a fierce battle in south-east Turkey with the BDP, and irrespective of the Turkish state's possible consideration that a more effective way to curtail ROJ-TV's influence on Turkey is to provide a Kurdish broadcast under state control, what matters is that fifteen years after Kurdish broadcasting began from Europe, what was once perceived to be impossible has now been realized: Kurdish-language broadcasting now also exists in Turkey.

Conclusion

While the future of ROJ-TV is uncertain in light of the ongoing pressure of the Turkish government and the competition of TRT 6, it can be safely maintained that it had a central role in nourishing and accelerating Kurdish mobilization both in Europe and in Turkey, as well as in breaking the monopoly of information on the Kurdish conflict that the Turkish military had established within the Turkish media. As the first Kurdish TV station ever, it not only enjoyed wide appeal among Kurdish viewers around the globe, it also presented a new challenge to the Turkish state, putting it severely under pressure with regard its own failure to meet the demands of its Kurdish population. Television became another battlefield of the Kurdish conflict, with ROJ-TV contesting Turkey everyday from afar, constituting a paradigmatic example for powerful transnational politics. So far, however, Kurdish diaspora politics have been rather disregarded in the literature when assessing Turkey's liberalizing reforms in the context of Europeanization. While scholarly debates on Turkey's reforms in the context of Europeanization have focused on the relationship of external and domestic factors, the example of Kurdish broadcasting shows that an analysis which takes immigrant and diaspora activities such as the Kurdish transnational political practices in Europe into account contributes for a more comprehensive understanding of recent political transformations in Turkey.

Notes

[1] I neither take the Kurdish transnational actors as the sole Kurdish actors putting pressure on the Turkish government nor do I underestimate the significance of the Kurdish domestic political movement in influencing the Turkish government's policies but rather focus particularly on the role of Kurdish transnational organizations for the present analysis.

[2] For the sake of readability, I refer to 'ROJ-TV' as the overarching name for the Kurdish satellite TV-station that was founded in 1995 as MED-TV, continued as MEDYA-TV and is since 2004 broadcasting under the name ROJ-TV. British and French authorities shut down the station in 1999 and 2004 (see further below), yet it reopened each time under a new name, while maintaining overall the same programming, staff and content.

[3] There is much speculation about the financing of ROJ-TV; indeed, this is one of the items that an ongoing Danish investigation against the station seeks to clarify. According to a Danish newspaper, since 2004 ROJ-TV has received 118,000,000 Danish Kr. (app. €16m) from the Copenhagen-based Kurdish Culture Foundation (KCF). The newspaper suggests that the funds from the KCF are illegal because there is no clarity as to how or from whom the KCF receives the money that it then donates: http://kurdistancommentary.wordpress.com/2010/09/07/case-overview-denmark-indicts-roj-tv-for-supporting-terrorism/ (accessed 10 September 2010).

[4] During 1990–1998, state security forces carried out a systematic depopulation policy in the rural areas of south-east Turkey, during which about two-thirds of the 5,000 villages and hamlets in the Kurdish region were destroyed or evacuated and more than one million Kurdish civilians displaced. For an analysis of the displacement of Kurds in Turkey see Ayata and Yükseker (2005); Kurban et al. (2007); Ayata (2011).

[5] While there are no empirical studies on the reception of ROJ-TV in Turkey available, it is safe to assert that ordinary Turkish citizens did not watch ROJ-TV since both the State and the Turkish media were presenting ROJ-TV as a station of the PKK, and it was insinuated that watching ROJ-TV was tantamount to supporting separatism. Within the Kurdish population, however, the appeal of ROJ-TV reached beyond ideological divisions, particularly when it was the only available Kurdish TV station. Today, however, there are more than a dozen Kurdish TV stations available broadcasting via satellite from Europe, Iran, and Iraq.

[6] http://en.firatnews.eu/index.php?rupel=article&nuceID=703 (accessed 5 September 2010).

[7] http://www.hurriyet.com.tr/english/domestic/11386242.asp?cr=1 (accessed 10 September 2010). However, former station director Manouchehr Zonoozi, went public in Spring 2010 stating that the station did, indeed, have connections with the PKK. He presented photographs of members of the ROJ-TV station management in a meeting with members of the PKK to the Danish police. ROJ-TV refutes these claims (http://en.firatnews.eu/index.php?rupel=article&nuceID=703 (accessed 10 September 2010)). On 31 August 2010, the Danish Prosecution Office issued an indictment against ROJ-TV for 'promoting the affairs of the terrorist organization, PKK'. For an overview of the Danish charges and the investigation against ROJ-TV in 2010, see http://kurdistancommentary.wordpress.com/2010/09/07/case-overview-denmark-indicts-roj-tv-for-supporting-terrorism/ (accessed 10 September 2010).

[8] The Danish Prime Minister Rasmussen had defended the publication of a cartoon in a Danish newspaper that was perceived to be offensive towards Muslims as a case of freedom of expression. For an overview of the Danish cartoon controversy, see Modood and Hansen (2006).

[9] See http://news.bbc.co.uk/2/hi/5380986.stm (accessed 10 September 2010).

[10] For a view of the Turkish government on this, see http://www.turkishweekly.net/news/68603/-39-rasmussen-is-an-unacceptable-name-for-nato-39-.html (accessed 10 September 2010).

[11] During my fieldwork, I visited the station in April 2006 and interviewed staff members and executive directors of that time. Ferda Cetin is no longer director of programming.

[12] Interview with Cetin, 28 April 2006. All following quotes in this section are from this interview.

[13] Already in June 2004, TRT began in one of its channels a daily thirty-minute broadcast in Kurdish, Zaza, Arabic, Bosnian, and Circassian. While this was certainly a critical moment for the broadcasting realities in Turkey, its impact was rather limited as the broadcast was very short.

[14] Atalay commented on the opening of TRT 6 by noting that 'for years, Kurdish was recorded in police records as an "unidentified language." They used to tell us that Kurds do not exist. Now they are going to tell us that there is no such thing as Kurds in Kurdish.' See http://www.todayszaman.com/detaylar.do?load=detay&link=162961 (accessed 5 September 2010). Atalay, the mayor of the city Batman, was convicted a few months later for having spoken Kurdish during the election campaign. Gülten Kisanak commented that Kurdish broadcast in the state television TRT was a strategy to actually contain further Kurdish demands, see http://bianet.org/bianet/ifade-ozgurlugu/110933-kisanak-trtde-kurtce-yayin-kurtlerin-taleplerini-bastirmak-icin (accessed 5 September 2010).

References

Ayata, B. (2008) Mapping Euro-Kurdistan, *Middle Eastern Report*, 38(247), pp. 18–24.
Ayata, B. (2011) *The Politics of Displacement: A Transnational Analysis of the Forced Migration of Kurds in Turkey and Europe* (USA: Johns Hopkins University, Department of Political Science).
Ayata, B. & Yükseker, D. (2005) A belated awakening: national and international responses to the internal displacement of Kurds in Turkey, *New Perspectives on Turkey*, 32, pp. 5–42.
Aydemir, Senay (2011, March 18). İki yilda 27 çalişani öldürüldü, *Radikal*.
Aytac, Ö. (2010, July 21) The democratic initiative and the Kurdish issue in Turkey since 2009, *Turkish Policy Quarterly*, pp. 101–116.
Barkey, H. J. & Fuller, G. E. (1998) *Turkey's Kurdish Question* (Lanham, USA: Rowman & Littlefield).
Cemal, H. (2003) *Kürtler* (Istanbul, Turkey: Dogan Kitap).
Christiansen, C. (2004) News media consumption among immigrants in Europe, *Ethnicities*, 4(2), pp. 185–207.
Ember, C. R., Ember, M. & Skoggard, I. (2004) *Encyclopedia of Diasporas: Immigrant and Refugee Cultures around the World* (New York and London: Kluwer Academic/Plenum).
Hale, W. (2003) Human rights, the European Union and the Turkish accession process, *Turkish Studies*, 4(1), pp. 107–126.
Hassanpour, A. (1998) Satellite footprints as national borders: MED-TV and the extraterritoriality of state sovereignty, *Journal of Muslim Minority Affairs*, 18(1), pp. 53–72.
Human Rights Watch (2010) *Protesting as a Terrorist Offense* (New York: HRW).
Kirisci, K. & Winrow, G. M. (1997) *The Kurdish Question and Turkey: An Example of a Trans-State Ethnic Conflict* (London, Portland: Routledge).
Kosnick, K. (2008) Exit and voice revisited: the challenge of migrant media, *Research Group Transnationalism Working Paper*, Number 9.
Kubicek, P. (2005) The European Union and grassroots democratization in Turkey, *Turkish Studies*, 6(3), pp. 361–377.
Kurban, D., Aker T., Celik A., Unalan T., Yükseker D. (2007) *Coming to Terms with Forced Migration: Post-Displacement Restitution of Citizenship Rights in Turkey* (Istanbul: TESEV Press).
Laciner, S. (2010, January 6) Bölücü Televizyon Yayinliciligi ve Uluslararasi Baglantilari: MED-TV Örnek Olayi (1994–1999), *Usakgündem*. Available at http://www.usak.org.tr/EN/myazdir.asp?id=329, last accessed November 10, 2010.
Lyon, A. J. & Ucarer, E. M. (2001) Mobilizing ethnic conflict: Kurdish separatism in Germany and the PKK, *Ethnic and Racial Studies*, 24(6), pp. 925–948.
McDowall, D. (2005) *A Modern History of the Kurds*, 3rd ed (London and New York: I. B. Tauris).
Modood, T. & Hansen, R. (2006) The Danish cartoon affair: free speech, racism, Islamism, and integration, *International Migration*, 44(5), pp. 3–62.
MRG (Minority Rights Group) (2007) *A Quest for Equality: Minorities in Turkey* (London: MRG).
Önis, Z. (2003) Domestic politics, international norms and challenges to the state: Turkey–EU relations in the post-Helsinki era, *Turkish Studies*, 4(1), pp. 9–34.
Romano, D. (2006) *The Kurdish Nationalist Movement: Opportunity, Mobilization and Identity* (Cambridge, UK and New York: Cambridge University Press).
Schimmelfennig, F., Engert S., Knobel H. (2003) Costs, commitment and compliance: the impact of EU democratic conditionality on Latvia, Slovakia and Turkey, *JCMS: Journal of Common Market Studies*, 41(3), pp. 495–518.
Van Bruinessen, M. (2000) *Transnational Aspects of the Kurdish Question* (Florence, Italy: European University Institute).
Zaman, A. (2009) *Winning Kurdish Hearts and Minds: The Battle Shifts to the Airwaves* (Washington, DC: German Marshall Fund).

The Post-westernisation of EU–Turkey Relations

HASAN TURUNÇ*
The School of Interdisciplinary Area Studies, University of Oxford, UK

ABSTRACT *This article examines an overly optimistic portrayal of the EU and its relationship with Turkey within the context of an essentialist framework for the dynamics of Turkish politics. It critically scrutinises conventional understandings of the dynamics of Turkey's domestic politics. It professes that relying upon outdated models of domestic political cleavages is not sufficient to understand the key dynamics of Turkey's EU accession process. The article analyses Turkey's interaction with Europe by incorporating, but also moving beyond, the narrow confines of dichotomous thinking: the West–East divide, modern versus traditional, global–local and secular pitted against Islamicist. Drawing upon the contemporary academic literature in Europe and Turkey, the article advances an alternative analytical perspective in order to understand better the dynamic changes within Turkey and Europe.*

Introduction

The European Union (EU) enlargement has traditionally been portrayed as simply a technical process of convergence by the candidate state with the EU institutions and the *acquis communautaire*—the corpus of EU laws and standards. EU integration is considered as the final destiny for the continent and each country, including non-EU states, is required to seek a place in the unfolding order. Analysing Turkey's journey towards the EU has suffered from the tendency to try to place political actors into one of two diametrically opposed groups: the modernising, secular and westernised Kemalist elites; and the emerging pro-Islamicist counter-elites who offer a conservative approach to social issues and a critical appraisal of the Kemalist project.

Prominent scholars on EU enlargement such as Thomas Diez (2004), Heinz Kramer (2006), Nathalie Tocci (2007), Paul Kubicek (2009) and Mehmet Ugur (2010) emphasise that Turkey's non-convergence with European norms puts the focus on Turkey as 'the other'. Turkey is exemplified as a prisoner of its geography, trapped between East and West, or expressed differently, its heart is in the East and its head is in the West. At best, it is seen as a bridge between East and West, which implies that Turkey is not rooted in Europe. However, the incompleteness of accounts built upon these foundations cannot simply be explained by Turkey's approach to the EU.

This article scrutinises an overly optimistic portrayal of the EU and its relationship with Turkey within the context of an essentialist framework for the dynamics of Turkish politics. It will critically examine conventional understandings of the dynamics of Turkey's domestic politics. It will profess that relying upon outdated models of domestic political cleavages is not sufficient to understand the key dynamics of Turkey's EU accession process. The article analyses Turkey's interaction with Europe by incorporating, but also moving beyond, the narrow confines of dichotomous thinking: the West–East divide, modern versus traditional, global–local and secular pitted against Islamicist. Drawing upon the contemporary academic literature in Europe and Turkey, the article will advance an alternative analytical perspective in order to better understand the dynamic changes within Turkey and Europe.

The article argues that we require a wider understanding of the socio-political changes in Turkey within the context of a changing Europe and a changing world. To this end it proposes the idea of post-westernisation or, more specifically, the idea that post-western Turkey is acting alongside a post-Cold War Europe. This is a Europe in which East and West are no longer solid reference points or identity markers, and in which a previously marginalised East has become central to political developments (Delanty, 2003).

Importantly, the 'post-westernisation framework', as sketched out by Gerard Delanty (2003, 2006), Goran Therborn (2006) and Chris Rumford (2008), enables us to attain a more sophisticated appreciation of the dynamics governing changes within, and between, Turkey and Europe using the post-westernisation lens. The article first will give an account of the prevailing theories and discuss changing circumstances in Turkish society and finally outline the new paradigm namely post-western Turkey.

An Outline of Prevailing Perspectives on EU–Turkey Relations

There is a great deal of scholarly work on Turkey's EU relations such as Ozbudun (2000), Kramer (2000), Keyman & Öniş (2004) and Öniş (2004). There are those who place the EU as central to the process of shaping and reshaping Turkish politics. Proponents of this line believe that after the Cold War Turkey has experienced a new wave of change that for the first time in recent history fundamentally questions the established principles of the Kemalist state tradition. They also emphasise the role of civil society in the emerging new foreign and security policy challenges. They argue that important changes have taken place in the recent period both in the nature of Turkish politics as well as the kind of signals provided by the EU. These changes have helped to push the momentum of economic and political reforms in Turkey thereby making the prospect of EU membership a stronger possibility. The EU has motivated Turkey to transform its state-centric polity into a more democratic, economically stable and pluralist one. This role has affected positively the process of consolidating Turkish democracy. Recent improvements in Turkey's democratic order would have been inconceivable without a strong EU support. The EU also assisted the development of civil society and its impact on the process of liberalising Turkish democracy.

On the other hand, there are those scholars who have a sceptical view of EU membership, questioning the catalytic role of the accession process in furthering democracy and human rights in Turkey. Typical among this group is Ahmet Evin (1994, pp. 13–23) who advocates the notion that during the Ottoman Turkish period, state elites in Turkey emphasised political leadership; following the transition to democracy in the mid-1940s, the situation was reversed and the stress was on political participation. Norman Stone (2005), alternatively, claims that the detailed and prescriptive corpus of EU rules and norms—known collectively as 'acquis communautaire' (acquis)—will impose an enormous unnecessary burden on the Turkish state yielding little to no tangible benefits:

> Can Turkey stand the unemployment, bureaucracy and taxation that the EU really portends? Up to the Turks. But there are those of us who might think that they can carry out the beneficial changes on their own and who might even say that, if they really want membership of the EU, they can have ours.

While, naturally, Evin and Stone, are not the only doubters of the positive externalities of Turkish accession, the mainstream sceptical view, notably articulated by Gunduz Aktan (European Rim Policy & Investment Council, 2003), conditionally accepts the accession process as long as the Republican pillars of unitary nationalism, strict secularism and the pre-eminence of the military in politics are not compromised by the requirements of the Copenhagen political criteria on democracy, civil liberties and human and minority rights.

There is also a sizeable body of scholarly work devoted to the rise of Islamicist politics in Turkey. Research in this area tends to concentre on indigenous cultural and political dynamics, interpreting the essence of Islamicist politics as the resurgence of a traditional culture which rejects market competition and capital accumulation (Barber, 1995). Modernisation itself is viewed as a uniquely western process rooted in the technologically and morally superior ways of accumulating wealth. Similarly, another perspective in this area focuses on the historical international dynamics of the political economy (McMichael, 2000) and global culture (Tomlinson, 1999) in the absence of a unified theoretical position. These scholars try to understand culture in broader terms as constitutive of globalisation wherein the global–local dynamics intersect and interconnect (Robertson & Khondker, 1998). According to their view, any attempt to explain religion in terms of the distinctive characteristics of a local culture misinterprets the complexity of globalisation. However, other scholars persist in viewing culture in terms of a dichotomy between the global and the local. This expects religion, seen as an element of a local culture, either to form a reactionary counter-movement against the global economy or to disappear with the expansion of market forces, telecommunication systems and computerised information networks. In particular, these scholars point to the intense cultural interactions marked by a tension between the homogenisation of the world and the resistance by local cultural differences.

In contrast to their expectations there was not a decline in the importance of Islam resulting from the expansion of the market economy. Far from disappearing from the political scene, however, Islam has emerged as a major player in Turkey's politics after the general elections results in 2002 (Ozcan & Turunc, 2011). Even if these studies, which privilege the division between local and global socio-economic and cultural factors, are synthesised, most of the arguments relating to modernisation and globalisation have limited utility in explaining the continuing importance of Islam in Turkey (Turunc, 2007). This is because many studies often associate the Islamicists, Justice and Development Party (JDP) with an oppressive tradition and violent anti-modern, anti-western social movements. Some scholars working on the rise of the JDP and Islam in general have offered explanations in line with those approaches. Gulalp (1997), for example, views the rise of Islamicist politics in Turkey since 1980 as a response to the frustration of the promises of modernisation under the impact of economic globalisation (Gulalp, 1997). According to Keyder (1997), however, the rise of political Islam owes its broadening appeal to the actual practice of limited modernisation, which did not expand political liberalism and citizenship rights in Turkey. Here, the emphasis is on the failure of the Turkish modernisation project known as Kemalism, central to the ideology of the Turkish Republic. As Kemalism fails to achieve its goal of modernisation, Islam tends to rise. In both explanations, the rise of Islam is understood as forming a resistance culture resulting from the failures of economic or cultural modernisation.

Gulalp views the oppositional character of Islam in terms of cultural globalisation and sees the rise of Islamist politics as part of this tendency of resistance to the homogenising effects of globalisation.

Barber (1995) and Gulalp (1997) interpreted the expansion of Islamic politics as the resurgence of a traditional culture suspicious of market competition and capital accumulation. Modernisation was viewed as a uniquely western process rooted in wealth creation and non-Islamic morality; the Islamicists generally were seen as an eastern, anti-modern social movement.

Unlike Barber, Gulalp added a cultural hue to the globalisation hypothesis on the spreading Islamicist polity. Naturally, Gulalp contends that such homogenising tendencies of cultural globalisation produced Islamicist distaste and disapproval manifested by identity politics reflective of the local world-views and cultures (Gulalp, 1997). Put differently, there is not one but multiple definitions of, and paths to, 'modernity' and Islamicism is one of them.

Keyder (1997) and Keyman and Öniş (2004) adopted a decidedly more socio-economic and political orientation to explain Islamicist developments. They maintained that political Islam owed its broadening appeal, in part, to the exclusion of economically disadvantaged groups from the benefits of globalisation. An added factor was the actual practice by the Kemalist establishment of constraining political liberalism and citizenship rights in Turkey at the behest of protecting the State's secular character. Islam is, therefore, essentially a vehicle of resistance emanating from the failures of restrained political participation aggravated by limited globalisation. On an identical strand of reasoning, Mardin (1997) notes that Islam establishes bridges between various groups because it provides a common cultural outlook shared by the upper and lower classes. Arguably, these bridges are built socially and politically by the state elite, including the civil and military bureaucrats and the political parties. In addition, Islamist ideology is fundamentally shaped by state administrators and political elites in response to domestic and international political and economic pressures (Ozcan & Turunc, 2008). After all, following the 1980 military coup, it was the decision of the civilian and military bureaucrats to restructure state organs and institutionalise liberal economic policies in Turkey while promoting Islam as a solution to contain the Left (Turunc, 2007).

Undoubtedly, the primary category of explanation, which arguably underpins the other two, concentrates on the collision and rivalry between two incompatible ideologies of Kemalism/secularism and Islamicism. This dialectical approach has, of course, undergone critical refinements and upgrading, acknowledging the post-Erbakan transformation in Islam, but is still attached to the bipolarity, and philosophical divergence and imbalance—as opposed to convergence and integration—as a contentious point of debate.

Gole (1996), Kramer (2000), Navaro-Yashin (2002), White (2003) and Yavuz (2003) are formidable proponents of such an approach, albeit with various lines of thought. While these thinkers recognise the differential revolution in Turkish Islam, and in some cases—such as Yavuz—portending that Turkish Islam is a distinctive, liberalising force in Turkey, none challenge, or at the very least hesitate to challenge, the underlying conflict-rooted premise of conflictual and dualistic understanding and interpretation of Turkish politics and society.

Those commentators and academics questioning the central notion of secularist-Islamist duality are rare. One possible exception is Tezel (2001, p. 47), who adheres indirectly to the traditional analysis, noting that:

> the outcome of the Turkish quest for civilisational transformation still depends on the courage and ingenuity of those citizens of Turkey loyal to the values of 'European political civilisation' in their competition with the other citizens of Turkey who aim at another kind of society with other set of values.

But, he attempts to reposition the debate from ideological dichotomy to divisions grounded on economic, geographic and educational determinants.

It is almost an article of faith in academia to view Turkey through lenses of conflict and division, especially between global and local, between modern and traditional and secularism and Islam. The next section will look into recent dynamics in Turkish society in order to comprehend fully the contemporary developments.

Conceptualisation of Post-westernisation

The majority of research on the EU integration deals with transition towards a Western European model and democratisation (Dahrendorf, 1990; Habermas, 1990; Diez, 2004; Tocci, 2007). However, a new theoretical approach towards understanding how Eastern European countries are responding to the transformation of Europe and at the same time how they are dealing with the restoration of their own societal order, a post-western outlook, is gradually emerging (Delanty, 2003; Wagner, 2004; Delanty & Rumford, 2005; Rumford, 2006a; Therborn, 2006). Post-westernisation is advocating a rewriting of the narratives of European integration with a view to opening new analytical approaches. The central pillar of the post-western framework is that Eastern Europe is changing at the same time continental Europe is changing, a transformational process which brings Eastern Europe and continental Europe closer and not just simply because of EU integration. It is argued that transformations shape Europe continuously. Within the contemporary order, these transformations are 'taking on a postwestern orientation in which a new east has emerged to shape Europe' (Delanty & Rumford, 2005, p. 24). Thus, 'Europe... is no longer divided along an East–West axis' (Rumford, 2006b, p. 2). Another key feature of post-westernisation is that, as opposed to a singular, homogenous and coherent entity, post-westernisation proposes to look at the West as a geopolitical space which is fragmented and lacks unity. Moreover, post-westernisation outlines the theme of 'multiple modernities' (Eisenstadt, 2000; Therborn, 2006; Delanty & Rumford, 2005), which suggests that modernity can no longer be theorised as a singular path of transformation. Therefore, a post-western Europe 'is a Europe that is no longer based on singular, western modernity, but multiple modernities' (Delanty & Rumford, 2005, p. 49). Consequently, Europe is best defined in terms of 'multiple modernities' (Eisenstadt, 2000; Therborn, 2003; Delanty & Rumford, 2005). Taking into account future EU enlargements, post-westernisation affirms that 'Europe is becoming more poly-centric, with more than one centre and also more than one historical origin' (Delanty & Rumford, 2005, p. 49) and that 'the identity of Europe will become more and more "postwestern"' (Delanty & Rumford, 2005, p. 47). Essentially, post-westernisation propagates a new analytical tool to analyse the West and suggests that a series of processes are taking place in which 'Europe is postwestern because it is no longer divided along an East–West axis, does not possess fixed Eastern borders, and accommodates multiple modernities' (Rumford, 2006b, p. 1). Those processes, arguably, lead to de-'unification of the West' and 'increasing lack of unity' within the western world.

Samuel Huntington (1996) labelled Turkey a 'torn country' at the civilisational fault line of separation and discord between two competing ideologies in which Islamicism is antithetical to alleged western 'imperialist' dominance, while Gellner (1994) describes Islam as an obstacle to the influx of European values, market competition and capital accumulation to protect localised cultural traditions. Within that conceptual framework, tension and polarisation determines the struggle between the 'global' and authentically 'local'. This dichotomy builds on a monolithic idea of modernity in which traditional and modern societies are two different opposing societal systems, each with contrasting set of features and values. While religious beliefs were local and located within the prism of the East, modern features included rationalism, universalism and individualism.

Nevertheless, the post-western dimension of integration marks the meeting point where Turkey and Europe convene at the end of the East–West division. One assumption for this integration dynamic is that a post-western 'Turkey meets a postwestern Europe' (Rumford, 2006b) built on 'multiple modernities'. First, post-western integration relates to the integration of Turkish society within wider transformations in Europe. Second, the post-western dimension of integration also concerns the transformative dimension of Europe affected itself by eastern transformations (Wagner, 2004). Put differently, post-western integration has transcended the boundaries of the Turkish society and has had a long-term impact not only on the Turkey's transformation but also on wider European transformations. Analysing post-western Turkey in a post-western Europe suggests the idea that Europe is changing at the same time Turkey is changing thereby Turkey is moving beyond the East–West distinction.

Therefore, it is more useful to understand Turkey by considering that it is going through a two-level integration. That is, on the one hand, an institutional level which includes the adaptation of the EU rules and *acquis communautaire* at a national level, and, on the other hand, at a societal level, towards becoming increasingly post-western. It is then argued that Turkey is integrating itself into a European order, which is itself undergoing major transformation. So, by looking at Turkey from a post-western perspective the relationship between Turkey and Europe gets a different dynamic than simply defining Turkey in terms of a linear process towards EU membership or located in the East. The next section will look at post-western elements in Turkey. The article will do so by adapting a critical approach to analyse Turkey through socio-economic cleavages which, arguably, undermines Turkey's EU vocation.

A Post-western Turkey

Carkoglu and Toprak (1999 and 2006) undertook two weighty surveys on secularism, religion and politics in 1999 and 2006 allowing us to hypothesise whether political Islam reflects the gathering absorption of secularism into—or its expulsion from—Turkish Islam.

There are quite a few academic publications, surveys and studies exploring specific areas of political Islam in Turkey with potentially important bearings on the contemporary accuracy of the dualistic theories and perceptions. Hazama (2003) has published articles exploring the relationship between voting patterns and cleavages in Turkey, additionally subjecting theories mentioned earlier, to rigorous scrutiny. Surveys conducted by Gallup in 2006 (Mogahed, 2006, pp. 1–3) and Pew Research Centre in 2005 (Speulda & McIntosh, 2004) and 2007 (Ruby, 2007) reveal insights into the mentality and orientation of Turks vis-à-vis Islam.

On the morally sensitive, nationally symbolic issue of the *türban* or the Islamic-style headscarf, Kalaycioglu (2005), for instance, used survey data to study whether not the attitudes towards the *türban* are closely related to religiosity and political Islam or rural values or other variables. Turkish pollster, A&G Araştırma Şirketi (2008) has done extensive and detailed surveys on sensitive social and political issues, ranging from secularism to the headscarf. Similar expansive and probative exercises on religion, society and democracy include the Kurdish-dominated south-eastern Turkey (Ergil, 2006).

Popular responses to secularism and the intermediary role played by Islamicist groupings—including *Tarikats* or spiritual brotherhoods—have received much attention by researchers. Tugal (2006) looked into the reasons underlying the growing effectiveness of Islamic movements by studying ethnographically the interaction between the religious movement and the people in a squatter district of Istanbul. The empirical analysis examined how the State and the Islamicists impact the lives of the residents, and how secularising and ritualising interventions are incorporated and resisted.

Publications indicate that institutional Islam is in the midst of a seemingly internally driven and comprehensive theological change. The Religious Directorates Office, or *Diyanet*, under the auspices of the progressive reformers of Ankara University's Faculty of Theology, is transforming systematically Sunni Islamic doctrine from a literalist, legalistic approach to interpretations based on contextualisation and identifying principles of morality conforming to the values of the twenty-first century (Donovan, 2006).

Along the road of reinterpretation of the Islamic holy texts or *Ijtihad*, 'misogynistic' *Hadith*, or sayings by Prophet Muhammed, are being deleted (Akyol, 2006) and *Qu'ranic* verses reinterpreted. This Islamic reform and its possible implications have barely witnessed much attention by commentators and experts with two exceptions. Bulent Ucar and German Jesuit Priest Felix Körner have released publications on these Islamic developments; the latter advises unofficially at the Faculty of Theology of Ankara University (Stahr, 2006).

'Muslim Reformation' has been the subject of field research in the central Anatolian city of Kayseri. Istanbul-based German think-tank, the European Stability Initiative, explored the 'quiet' changes and 'pro-business currents' within Turkish Islam and how Anatolian businesspeople—and key backers of the JDP party—or 'Islamic Calvinists' marry piety with global capitalism using the *Nursi Tarikat* to foster commercial networks and community-based initiatives (European Stability Initiative, 2005, pp. 1–41). On the basis of such work, one can argue that in order to form an effective analysis of the rise of Islamic politics and societal changes unfolding in Turkey, one needs to go beyond the explanations based on globalisation studies or secularism–Islam conflict. Islamicist politics did not suddenly emerge in the 1980s as a new social movement under the conditions of globalisation. It has its roots in the nineteenth-century Pan-Islamicist movement structure in ways far more complex than is often assumed. The Ottoman Empire and the Turkish state were actively involved in shaping the role of Islam in politics.

Undoubtedly, Islam lies at the heart of Turkey's evolving identity defining two, perhaps even three, of the traditional identifiable cleavages of Turkish society, namely: Secularist/Kemalist—Islamicist and Sunni—Alevi dichotomies, and less so the Turkish Sunni *Hanafi* versus Kurdish *Shafi'* division. Dimitris Keridis (2004, p. 329) observed that the Turkish reality has often been conceptualised in terms of dualities and antitheses, cogently described by Serif Mardin's seminal 1970s formulation of Turkish politics and society within the prism of centre–periphery relations (Mardin, 1973). He considers that the Islamic movements exhibited growing resistance to the Turkish modernisation project since the social and political reforms of the last eighty years propagated by the Kemalist elites have alienated and distanced the majority of conservative Muslims in Turkey (Mardin, 1997).

Notwithstanding the major changes swirling through political Islam, the dominant viewpoint remains that the dialectical framework, while necessitating updating and refinement, is most suited to the context of Turkey.

One can observe that the traditional framework accentuates the assumed divergence and conflict as opposed to cross-fertilisation and integration between political Islam and secularism, and conceives the variable balance between them in zero-sum terms: the gains of one ideology corresponds to the losses of the other. The conflict-ridden period of Turkish history subsequent to the establishment of the modern republic in 1923 punctuated by periodic military coups seems to lend credence to the viability of the dual and conflictual theories as an effective analytical and explanatory tool to comprehend political Islam–secularist relational dynamics in Turkey.

Yet, at a basic level, those dualistic theories mentioned above appear unable to assess fully the complete changeover in crucial aspects of Turkish political Islam, ranging from embracing EU accession to endorsing a radical free market agenda and globalisation. An analysis of EU–Turkey relations and the JDP's rise needs to go beyond the conception of modern versus tradition or secularism versus Islam. This is illustrated by the fact that the JDP was a 'big tent' of the Anatolian business and peasant communities, urban poor, Kurds and, refreshingly, liberal voters—17.7 per cent of JDP's constituency are self-described 'Ataturk's followers' and 18.1 per cent describe themselves as 'modern' (Akgun, 2007, p. 205). This party, in other words, represented a new political force in Turkish politics with a broad appeal to the former centre-right, centre, nationalist, as well as a portion of Islamicist voters (Ozbudun, 2000).

The underlying premise of such dualistic and antithetical theories is conflict and division between a modernising, secularising elite and a traditional, pious population. Its corollary is that the emerging 'Muslim bourgeoisie', the urban poor and the Anatolian populace imbued with deep religiosity aim to assert a rightful claim to the power and privileges enjoyed by the Kemalist elite—defined as self-appointed successors of the Kemal Ataturk's legacy who are ardent secularists or supporters of French-style *laïcité* suspicious of any manifestations of religious observance in public and social life. And this supposed Islamicist demand—denoting a tradition under which Islam is seen as all-embracing, and hence properly the origin and inspiration of political ideas—embodies inevitable tension with the secularist forces, namely the 'White Turk' business elite, the judiciary and, most important of all, the Turkish military.

Turkey's changing foreign relations are also evidence of the post-westernisation of Turkey, or perhaps to put it more accurately Turkey's emerging post-western foreign policy on Iraq, Russia, China, Afghanistan, USA and the Middle East and North Africa. There is a plethora of scholarly and non-scholarly work on the re-orientation of Turkish foreign policy, but none matches post-westernisation in explicating Turkish foreign relations. For example, Turkey originally had stable relations with western countries such as the USA, UK and France within the framework of various westerns institutions, for example NATO, OECD, whereas now there are also burgeoning relations with the Middle East, Russia and China. The post-western foreign policy is defined by shifting alliances between East and West depending on the strategic issues. Turkey's foreign policy is no longer determined by simple Cold-War Manichean alliances. It is now characterised by multi-faceted, shifting and interest-based alliances as opposed to ideological and cohesive partnerships. This is evidenced by several recent incidents such as opposing western sponsored UN sanctions on Iran, initially rejecting NATO's intervention in Libya and Syria and deteriorating relations with long-time ally Israel.

Conclusion

It can be observed that the current academic scholarship and commentary is not offering novel insights into Turkey and EU in the flux of continuous change. Research by Rumford (2006a and 2006b), Rumford & Turunc (2011) and Turunc (2011) has laid bare the limitations of the analytical tools and knowledge-base of current approaches and studies undermined by a western-focused, historically deterministic angle to appraising country and international phenomena. Turkey simply does not fit neatly within these academic models. Post-westernisation, on the other hand, as the name implies, attempts to capture the 'true' face of Europe, an area of multiplying identities, fragmenting loyalties united by a 'cosmopolitan', universal values of human rights, democratic legitimacy, environmental consciousness and popular accountability of government initiatives. It underscores, under the rubric of 'critical cosmopolitanism', that Europe is not a singular entity, but a composite of universal values, cultural traditions and regional identities where the West in general and Europe in particular is no longer the main reference point of identity formation. In an interdependent world, in which a unipolar system of super power magnitude is diversifying into a multipolar orientation, Europe and the West is now only one of the important players, as opposed to the sole or dominant, player in the post-Cold War period. A glaring void was surfacing in academic theories and disciplines adapted to a pre-Cold War era as a result of a changeover in global affairs; encouragingly, post-westernisation is filling that gap.

Much like Europe, Turkey is moving away from a singular identity fostered by one power elite into a kaleidoscope of identities and modernities. No longer are Kemalists predominant in politics and the economy. State and society are leaving behind the simplicity of the past and replacing it with the uncertainties and richness of multiple layers of cultures, opinions and ideologies. Turkey is not defined by one elite but by many elites, old and new, which are themselves changing and adapting to globalisation. Gone is the interventionist, titular secularism of yesteryear replaced by varied definitions of separating religion from state. Post-westernisation provides another framework to appreciate the change from 'old' Turkey to the 'new' Turkey, but at the level of the State; conceptual elasticity is at the core of post-westernism. Kemalism is not the sole source of legitimacy but one of many principles competing in contemporary Turkey.

By defining the shifting sands in the EU and Turkey, post-westernisation, naturally, proffers an explicatory paradigm for the EU–Turkey accession dynamic. Accession to the EU is not reducible to the implementation of the *acquis communautaire*, economic liberalisation and institutional upgrading; the EU is much more than that. It is a set of values enunciated by the Copenhagen Criteria, about a better quality of life, about integrating with the world via trade, investments and global civic action, about European 'soft power' inspiring a society to internalise civil liberties with responsibility. That is what Europe is becoming to Turkey: a catalyst for democratic change, a promoter of the rule of law, a guarantor of secularism and consolidator of democracy, a mechanism that disciplines wayward behaviour, a guide to a modernity rooted neither in a single geography nor ideology and both East and West.

References

A&G Araştırma Şirketi (2008) *Tum arastirmalarimiz*. Available online at: http://www.agarastirma.com.tr/tumarastirma.asp (accessed 4 April 2010).

Akgun, B. (2007) *Turkiye'de Secmen Davranisi Sistemi ve Sosyal Guven* (Ankara: Nobel).

Akyol, M. (2006, July 16) '[Sexism deleted] in Turkey', *Washington Post*. Available online at: http://www.washingtonpost.com/wp-dyn/content/article/2006/07/14/AR2006071401381.html (accessed 14 January 2012).

Barber, B. (1995) Jihad vs. McWorld: How Globalism and Tribalism Are Reshaping the World (New York: Balantine Books).

Carkoglu, A., & Toprak, B. (1999) *Türkiye'de Din, Toplum ve Siyaset* [Religion, Politics, Society in Turkey] (TESEV Yayınları).

Carkoglu, A., & Toprak, B. (2006) *Türkiye'de Din, Toplum ve Siyaset* [Religion, Politics, Society in Turkey] (TESEV Yayınları).

Dahrendorf, R. (1990) *Reflections on the Revolution in Europe* (London: Chatto and Windus).

Delanty, G. (2003) The making of a post-western Europe: a civilizational analysis, *Thesis Eleven*, 72(1), pp. 8–25.

Delanty, G. and Rumford, C. (2005) *Rethinking Europe: Social Theory and the Implications of Europeanization* (London: Routledge).

Delanty, G. (2006) *Europe and Asia beyond East and West* (London: Routledge).

Diez, T. (2004) Europe's others and the return of geopolitics, *Cambridge Review of International Affairs*, 17(2), pp. 319–335.

Donovan, J. (2006) Turkey: Islamic reformers look back to future, *RadioFreeEurope*, 29 November. Available online at: http://www.rferl.org/featuresarticle/2006/11/337875B4-9662-4F19-A0DD-1935BA70E7B1.html (accessed 29 December 2010).

Eisenstadt, S. N. (2000) Multiple modernities, *Daedalus*, 129(1), pp. 1–29.

Ergil, D. (2006) Results of a survey conducted in 2005 on democracy in Turkey. *European Journal of Turkish Studies*, Thematic Issue no. 5. Available online at: http://www.ejts.org/document769.html (accessed 3 March 2010).

European Rim Policy and Investment Council (2003) Interview with Gunduz Aktan, *Perihelion Interviews*. Available online at: http://www.erpic.org/old/perihelion/interviews/aktan.htm#_edn1 (accessed 21 August 2010).

European Stability Initiative (2005) Islamic Calvinists: change and conservatism in central Anatolia, *European Stability Initiative*, 19 September, Berlin–Istanbul. Available online at: http://www.esiweb.org/pdf/esi_document_id_69.pdf (accessed 20 October 2010).

Evin, A. (1994) Demilitarization and civilianization of the regime, in: A. Evin & M. Heper (Eds) *Politics in the Third Turkish Republic: Transition to Democracy* (Boulder, CO: Westviews Press), pp. 23–39.

Gellner, E. (1994) *Conditions of Liberty: Civil Society and Its Rivals* (New York: Penguin Books).

Gole, N. (1996) Authoritarian secularism and Islamist politics, in: A. R. Norton (Ed.) *Civil Society in Middle East* (Leiden and Boston, MA: Brill Academic Publishers), pp. 17–43.

Gulalp, H. (1997) Globalising postmodernism: Islamist and western social theory, *Economy and Society*, 26(3), pp. 419–433.

Habermas, J. (1990) *Moral Consciousness and Communicative Action* (Cambridge: MIT Press).

Hazama, Y. (2003) Social cleavages and electoral support in Turkey: toward convergence? *The Developing Economies*, 41(3), pp. 362–387.

Huntington, S. P. (1996) *The Clash of Civilizations and the Remaking of World Order* (New York: Simon & Schuster).

Kalaycioglu, E. (2005) The mystery of the turban: participation or revolt? *Turkish Studies*, 6(2), pp. 233–251.

Keridis, D. (2004) Foreign strategies and domestic choices: balancing between power politics and interdependence, in: G. M. Lenore & D. Keridis (Eds) *The Future of Turkish Foreign Policy* (Cambridge: MIT Press), pp. 321–334.

Keyder, C. (1997) Whither the project of modernity, in: S. Bozdogan & R. Kasaba (Eds) *Rethinking Modernity and National Identity in Turkey* (Seattle, WA and London: University of Washington Press), pp. 37–51.

Keyman, F. & Öniş, Z. (2004) Helsinki, Copenhagen and beyond: challenges to the new Europe and the Turkish state, in: M. Uğur & N. Canefe (Eds) *Turkey and European Integration: Accession Prospects and Issues* (London: Routledge), pp. 173–194.

Kramer, H. (2000) *A Changing Turkey: The Challenge to Europe and the United States* (Washington, DC: Brookings Institution Press).

Kramer, H. (2006) Turkey and the EU: the EU's perspective, *Insight Turkey*, 8(4), pp. 24–32.

Kubicek, P. (2009) The European Union and political cleavages in Turkey, *InsightTurkey*, July, pp. 109–126.

Mardin, S. (1973) Centre-periphery relations: a key to Turkish politics? *Daedadus*, 102(Winter), pp. 169–190.

Mardin, S. (1997) Projects as methodology: some thought on modern Turkish social science, in: S. Bozdogan & R. Kasaba (Eds) *Rethinking Modernity and National Identity in Turkey*, pp. 64–80 (Seattle, WA: University of Washington Press).

McMichael, M. (2000) *Development and Social Change: A Global Perspective (Sociology for a New Century Series)* (Thousand Oaks, CA: Pine Forge Press).

Mogahed, D. (2006) Perspectives of women in the Muslim world, *Gallup Muslim ThinkForum*, 6 June. Available online at: http://media.gallup.com/WorldPoll/PDF/PerspectivesOfWomenInTheMuslimWorld.pdf (accessed 25 February 2010).

Navaro-Yashin, Y. (2002) *Faces of the State: Secularism and Public Life in Turkey* (Princeton: Princeton University Press).

Öniş, Z. (2004) Turkish modernization and challenges for the new Europe, *Perceptions*, 9(3), pp. 1–23.

Ozbudun, E. (2000) *Contemporary Turkish Politics: Challenges to Democratic Consolidation* (Colorado and London: Lynne Reinner Publishers).

Ozcan, G. B. & Turunc, H. (2008) The politics of administrative decentralization in Turkey since 1980, in: J. Killian & N. Eklund (Eds) *Handbook of Administrative Reform: An International Perspective* (Boca Raton, FL, London and New York: CRC Press), pp. 170–194.

Ozcan, G. & Turunc, H. (2011) Economic liberalisation and class dynamics in Turkey: new business groups and Islamic mobilisation since the 1980s, *InsightTurkey*, 13(3), pp. 63–86.

Robertson, R. & Khondker, H. H. (1998) Discourses of globalization: preliminary considerations, *International Sociology*, 13(March), pp. 25–40.

Ruby, R. (2007) Can secular democracy survive in Turkey? Turmoil over a presidential choice highlights Turks' concerns about religious influence in political life, *Pew Forum on Religion & Public Life*, released 4 May. Available online at: http://pewresearch.org/pubs/470/can-secular-democracy-survive-in-turkey (accessed 20 March 2010).

Rumford, C. (2006a) Introduction: theorizing borders, *European Journal of Social Theory*, 9(2), pp. 155–169.

Rumford, C. (2006b) Rethinking Turkey's relationship with the EU: postwestern Turkey meets postwestern Europe, *Politics and International Relations Working Paper*, No. 3, November.

Rumford, C. (2008) *Cosmopolitan Spaces: Europe, Globalization, Theory* (New York and London: Routledge).

Rumford, C. & Turunc, H. (2011) Postwesternisation: a framework for understanding Turkey–EU relations, in: A. Emre Cakir (Ed.) *Fifty Years of EU–Turkey Relations* (London and New York: Routledge), pp. 136–158.

Speulda, N. & McIntosh, M. (2004) Global gender gaps, *The Pew Global Attitudes Project*, released 13 May. Available online at: http://pewglobal.org/commentary/display.php?AnalysisID=90 (accessed 18 February 2010).

Stahr, V. S. (2006) Turkey as a laboratory of Islam? Synthesis of Islamic thought, secularism and modernity [trans. from the German by P. Anderson], *Neue Zürcher Zeitung*, 7 September. Available online at: http://www/qantara.de/webcom/show_article.php/_c-575/_nr-16/_p-1/i.html?PHPSESSID= (accessed 2 February 2010).

Stone, N. (2005, October 3) Energetic, honest and transformed—so why does Turkey need us anyway? *TimesOnline*. Available online at: http://www.timesonline.co.uk/tol/comment/columnists/guest_contributors/article573995.ece (accessed 5 March 2008).

Tezel, Y. S. (2001) Tale of two Turkeys, *Internationale Politik—Transatlantic Edition*, 1/2001, 2(Spring), pp. 47–53.

Therborn, G. (2006) Post-Western Europe and the plural Asias, in: G. Delanty (Ed.) *Europe and Asia beyond East and West: Towards a New Cosmopolitanism* (London: Routledge), pp. 24–44.

Tocci, N. (2007) *EU and Conflict Resolution: Promoting Peace in the Backyard* (New York: Routledge/UACES Contemporary European Studies).

Tomlinson, J. (1999) *Globalisation and Culture* (Chicago, IL: The University of Chicago Press).

Tugal, C. Z. (2006) The appeal of Islamist politics: ritual and dialogue in a poor district of Turkey, *The Sociological Quarterly*, 47(2), pp. 245–273.

Turunc, H. (2007) Islamicist or democratic? The AKP's search for identity in Turkish politics, *Journal of Contemporary European Studies*, 15(1), pp. 79–91.

Turunc, H. (2011) *The Democratic Transition in Turkey: The Transformation of Civil Society and the Challenges of EU Accession* (London: I.B. Tauris).

Ugur, M. (2010) Open-ended membership prospect and commitment credibility: explaining the deadlock in EU–Turkey accession negotiations, *Journal of Common Market Studies*, 48(4), pp. 967–991.

Wagner, P. (2004) Sonderweg Romania? in: H. F. Carey (Ed.) *Romania since 1989: Politics, Economics and Society* (Oxford: Lexington Books), pp. 49–67.

White, J. (2003) *Islamist Mobilization in Turkey: A Study in Vernacular Politics* (Seattle, WA and London: University of Washington Press).

Yavuz, H. (2003) *Islamic Political Identity in Turkey: Religion and Global Politics* (Oxford and New York: Oxford University Press).

Index

Note: Page numbers in *italic* type refer to tables
Page numbers followed by 'n' refer to notes

acquis communautaire 79, 82, 86
Akcapar, B. 61
Aksoy, T. 23
Aktan, G. 79
Amnesiac history 33
Anamnesis 32, 40–1
Ankara Criteria 8, 21
Ankara University: Faculty of Theology 83
Antiquarian history 33, 35–9
Ashley, R.K. 44
Ataturk, M.K. 34, 35, 36, 37–8, 84
Ayata, B. 3, 65–75
Aydin, C. 11

Bakhtin, M.: dialogism and EU-Turkey relations 3, 43–51, 50n
Barber, B. 80
Behnan, E. 35–6, 39
Berlin Plus 50n
Birdal, A. 23
Blockmans, S. 47
Bonnett, A. 44
Bruinessen, M. Van 57
Buhari-Gulmez, D. 2, 17–29
Büyükkaya, A. 23

Carkoglu, A.: and Toprak, B. 82
Çatalpinar, S. 17
Cayhan, E. 54
Cemal, H. 69
Central Asia 58
Çetin, F. 70–1
Çetin, İ. 22
civil society 78
civilization 11
civilizationalist perspective 11–12; binary 11; Occidentalist 11; syncretic 11
Common Security and Defence Policy (CDSP) 46–7
constitutional reform 9
Cornell, S.E. 57
Critical history 33
curriculum: national history *see* national history curriculum
Cyprus 43, 60

Davutoğlu, A. 12, 13
Delanty, G. 78
Demirel, S. 58, 66
Democrat Party (DP) 7
democratization narrative: Justice and Development Party (AKP) 7–10; people notion 8; veiling 8–9
Denmark: and ROJ-TV 70
depopulation policy 74n
dialogism: EU-Turkey dialogic relationship 48–50; and EU-Turkey relations 43–51; explanation 44–6; negotiations without dialogue 46–7; utterance concept 45, 46
Diamandouros, N. 23
Diez, T. 77
Dilek, M.S. 25
displacement: Kurds 74n
Durna, M. 17–18

emergency: state of 56–9
Erbakan, N. 8, 10, 58, 60
Erdoğan, R.T. 8, 9, 11, 66; European Association of History Educators (EUROCLIO) 34, 41
European Court of Human Rights (ECHR) 9
European Stability Initiative 83
European Union Military Staff (EUMS) 47
Europeanization 17–29; goodness of fit models 18–19, 26; macro-sociological insights 19–20; Ombudsmanship reform 20–5; sender-receiver models 18, 26
Evin, A. 78–9
Evren, K. 56

Fisher Onar, N. 2, 5–15, 49
forgetting: importance 32–5
France 46
Freedom House 22

INDEX

Gaza flotilla raid (2010) 12
Gellner, E. 82
George Eckert Institute 41n
Germany 46
Gole, N. 80
goodness of fit models: Europeanization 18–19, 26
Guillaume, X. 44, 45, 48, 50n
Gül, A. 11
Gül, H. 9
Gulalp, H. 79–80

Hacaloğlu, A. 23
Hamas 12
Hazama, Y. 83
headscarf ban 9, 83
Helsinki Summit (1999) 59
historical institutionalism: and Turkey-EU relations 3, 53–63; and unintended consequences 55, 56, 59
history: relationship of modes to past 33
history curriculum *see* national history curriculum
human rights 60, 67
Humanitarian Relief Foundation (IHH) 12
Huntington, S. 82

Icoz, G. 3, 53–63
Ijitihad 83
illocutionary acts 6, 7
Independent Commission on Turkey 43
institutionalism: rational choice 54, 55; sociological 54, 55
Islamic Law 10, 60
Islamicism: and politics 79–85
Israel 12

Johansson-Nogues, E.: and Jonasson, A-K. 43
Justice and Development Party (AKP) 5–15, 61, 72, 73, 79, 83, 84; democratization narrative 7–10; Ottomanist narrative 12–13; post-Islamist narrative 10–12; Turkey Inc narrative 13–14

Kalaycioglu, E. 83
Kemalism 80, 84, 85
Keridis, D. 84
Keyder, C. 80
Kosnick, K. 70
Kramer, H. 77, 80
Krasner, S. 56, 60
Kubicek, N. 77
Kurdish conflict 11, 12, 38, 57–8, 60, 65–75; transnational European diaspora activism 67–8
Kurdish Human Rights Project (KHRP) 67

Kurdish language 66, 68, 72, 74n
Kurdish Students Society in Europe (KSSE) 67
Kurdistan 57
Kurdistan Workers' Party (PKK) 57, 58, 65, 67, 68, 69, 70, 71
Kurds: displacement 74n
Kurds, The (Cemal) 69

Laciner, S. 71; *et al* 54
Luxembourg Summit (1997) 59

mahalle baskısı 9
Mardin, S. 80, 84
Maresceau, M. 46
Menderes, A. 7, 8
Merkel, A. 46
Merton, R.K. 55–6, 59
modernization 79–80
Monologism 46, 48
Monumental history 32, 35–9
Motherland Party (ANAP) 56

national history curriculum 31–42, 41n; Amnesiac history 33; Antiquarian history 33, 35–7; Critical history 33, 37–9; First World War 37; and forgetting 32–5; history uses 32–5; Monumental history 33, 35–7; Ottoman Empire 38; religion 39; Treaty of Sèvres (1920) 39–40
National Security Council (MGK) 53–63; emergency rule support 56–9; power curtailment and negotiations 59–61
National Unity and Fraternity Project 66
National View (MG) movement 10, 12
Nationalist Action Party (CHP) 23
Navaro-Yashin, Y. 80
neo-Ottomanism 6
Neumann, I.B. 44, 48
Nietzsche, F. 3, 31–42; Amnesiac history 33, 37–9; Antiquarian history 33, 35–7; Critical history 33, 37–9; forgetting 32–5; history uses 32–5; Monumental history 32, 35–7
North Atlantic Treaty Organization (NATO) 47
Nykänen, J. 3, 43–51

Ocalan, A. 58, 60–1
ombudsmanship 17–29; *muhtesip* 25; national variations 20–1; opposition 23–4; Ottoman origins 23–4, 25; parliamentary debates 22–3; survey findings 24–5; Turkish reform 21–5
opportunity costs 43
Oran, B. 60–1

INDEX

Ottomanist narrative: Justice and Development Party (AKP) 12–13; nostalgia 12
Ozal, T. 56–7, 58, 66
Özbudan, E. 22
Özgür Gündem 68–9

path dependence 53, 55
Pazarci, H. 23
Peace and Democracy Party (BDP) 23, 24
perlocutionary effects 7, 9, 12
Peters, B.G.: *et al* 56
Petersburg Declaration (1992) 47
Phillips, D. 21
Pierson, P. 55; and Skocpol, T. 54
politics: and Islamicism 79–85
post-Islamist narrative: Justice and Development Party (AKP) 10–12
post-westernization: conceptualization 81–2; framework 77–88; integration 82–3
punctuated equilibrium 53, 56

Rasmussen, A.F. 70, 74n
rational choice institutionalism 54, 55
Refik, A. 35–6, 37
Religious Directorates Office 83
Republican People's Party (CHP) 22
rights: human 60, 67
ROJ-TV 66, 67, 68, 74n; challenging Turkey 68–9; diaspora activism 67–8; and EU candidacy 72–3; and European norm diffusion 70–2; state power evasion and transnationalism 69–70
Rumford, C. 78, 81, 85

Şahin, L. 9
Şahin, M. 8
Salah ad-Din 39
Sarkozy, N. 46
Saydam, A. 40, 41n
secularism 80–1, 82–3, 84
sender-receiver models: Europeanization 18, 26
Sevinc, K. 43, 49
Sèvres: Treaty (1920) 39–40
Sewell, W.H. 55
Sezen, S. 26
Shapiro, M.J. 44
Shar'ia Law 10, 60
Skinner, Q. 7
Skocpol, T.: and Pierson, P. 54
sociological institutionalism 54, 55
Soviet Union: collapse 58
speech act theory 6, 14

state of emergency 56–9
state power evasion 69–70
State Supervisory Council 22
Steinmo, S.: and Thelen, K. 56
Stone, N. 79
strategic depth doctrine 12, 13
Stubb, A. 49, 50n

Tanrikulu, A.K. 25
Tarikats 83
Tezel, Y.S. 81
Thelen, K.: and Steinmo, S. 56
Therborn, G. 78
Tocci, N. 77
Toprak, B. 9–10; and Carkoglu, A. 82
transnationalism 69–70
Transparency International 22
Tugal, C.Z. 83
Turkey Inc narrative: Justice and Development Party (AKP) 13–14
Turkish Constitutional Court 22
Turkish Grand National Assembly (TBMM) 56, 57, 59, 60
Turkish Industrialists and Businessman's Association (TUSIAD) 22
Turkish Radio and Television Corporation (TRT) 66, 72, 73
Turunç, H. 3, 77–88

Ugur, M. 77
Union of Chambers and Commodity Exchanges of Turkey (TOBB) 22
Uras, U. 24, 25
utterance 45, 46; addressivity 45

Vachudova, M.A. 55
veiling 8–9

Webb, E. 3, 31–42
Welfare Party (RP) 59, 61
Western European Union (WEU) 47
White, J. 80

Yavuz, H. 80–1
Yazgan, H. 17, 24
Yilmaz, M. 59

Zana, L. 66
Zonoozi, M. 74n

www.routledge.com/9780415615327

Related titles from Routledge

Turkey and the EU: Accession and Reform
Edited by Gamze Avci and Ali Çarkoğlu

This volume is a comprehensive, state of the art study of domestic politics and policies and their role in Turkey's EU accession. The content is structured along issues, dynamics, actors and policies that drive Turkish politics and it provides an integrated assessment of the dynamics in Turkey-EU relations to general readers, students and specialists in EU Enlargement and Turkish politics alike.

Original contributions to 'classic' topics such as the customs union, human rights, military, civil society, public and elite opinion, political parties and the Kurdish issue are made by assessing the domestic sources of recent developments during the negotiations period. In addition, 'new' topics are included that previously have not been covered or analysed in volumes on Turkish-EU relations such as the Alevi issue, European Turks, corruption in Turkey, and Turkish parliamentary elite opinion on Turkey and the EU.

This book was published as a special issue of *South European Society and Politics*.

August 2012: 246 x 174: 320pp
Hb: 978-0-415-615327
£85 / $140

For more information and to order a copy visit
www.routledge.com/9780415615327

Available from all good bookshops

www.routledge.com/9780415466196

Related titles from Routledge

Turkey's Road to European Union Membership:
National Identity and Political Change
Edited by S. Verney and K. Ifantis

Enlargement to Turkey is one of the greatest challenges facing the European Union. After the narrowly averted "train crash" over Cyprus in 2006, the second election victory of the Justice and Development Party in July 2007 opened new prospects for Turkish-EU relations. But in an EU emphasising a collective identity based on shared civilisational values, Turkey's European credentials have been increasingly called into question.

This volume examines the EU role in strengthening the domestic pro-reform coalition within Turkey, the paradox - and potential limits - of Turkey's europeanising Islamists, and the impact of Europeanisation through conditionality, including a case study of Turkish policy towards the Cyprus Question.

This book was previously published as a special issue of the *Journal of Southern Europe and the Balkans*

August 2008: 246 x 174: 144pp
Hb: 978-0-415-466196
£90 / $155

For more information and to order a copy visit
www.routledge.com/9780415466196

Available from all good bookshops

www.routledge.com/9780415693912

Related titles from Routledge

Turkish Immigrants in Western Europe and North America: Immigration and Political Mobilization

Edited by Sebnem Koser Akcapar

Public and even scholarly debates usually focus on the integration problems of Muslim immigrants, at the cost of overlooking the role of the growing number of migrant organizations in establishing a crucial link among immigrants themselves, as well as between them and their countries of origin and residence. This book aims to fill a gap in the vast literature on migration from Turkey by contributing to the neglected aspect of civic and political participation of Turkish immigrants. It brings together a number of scholars who carried out extensive research on the associational culture of Turkish immigrants living in different countries in Europe and North America. In order to understand the diversity and dynamics within Turkish migrant communities living in these parts of the world yet maintaining transnational ties, this book offers a comparative and interdisciplinary approach to migrant organizations in general and civic participation and political mobilization of Turkish immigrants in particular.

This book was published as a special issue in *Turkish Studies*.

February 2012: 234 x 156: 200pp
Hb: 978-0-415-693912
£85/$145

For more information and to order a copy visit
www.routledge.com/9780415693912

Available from all good bookshops